FINDING VICTORY

WHEN HEALING DOESN'T HAPPEN

BREAKING THROUGH WITH HEALING PRAYER

Randy Clark & Craig Miller

globalawakening
lighting fires • building bridges • casting vision

1451 Clark Street, Mechanicsburg, PA 17055

ENDORSEMENTS

Finding Victory When Healing Doesn't Happen: Breaking Through with Healing Prayer is a book inspired by the Holy Spirit! I was moved and inspired by its redemptive insights. The testimonies held so much truth and living water within them I could not put this book down. Dr. Randy and Craig have been anointed with the Gift of Healing and the knowledge of the stumbling blocks when healing does not take place. By beginning at the beginning, the core of illness, your own life experiences can be a cause…Trust and Believe!

KAREN JASZCZALT, RN
VP of Clinical Services, Forest Health Medical Center

There are a plethora of reasons why healing does not seem to come to everyone. We rejoice immensely in the ones that receive their healing. Our hearts go out to those who continue to wait and seek for their healing which as yet, has not yet come. Dr. Randy Clark and Craig Miller, both very experienced in praying for the sick with amazing results, share their insights into what can hinder and block the amazing grace of God's healing power. This book is desperately needed as a resource for all of us who want to see God's kingdom come in his will be done on earth as it is in heaven.

JOHN ARNOTT
Catch the Fire, Toronto

"My heart breaks for all the sick Christians who have prayed for years with no visible results. They silently cry to God, 'Why?' Now we have the answers.

SID ROTH
Host, "It's Supernatural!"

FINDING VICTORY WHEN HEALING DOESN'T HAPPEN

BREAKING THROUGH WITH HEALING PRAYER

Randy Clark & Craig Miller

Apostolic Network of Global Awakening
1451 Clark Street
Mechanicsburg, PA 17055

For more information on how to order this book or any of the other materials that Global Awakening offers, please contact the Global Awakening Bookstore.

ISBN: 978- 1-937467-81-4

Second printing April 2015

TABLE OF CONTENTS

FOREWORD

It has been my joy to travel the world with my parents, Charles and Frances Hunter for over 30 years and now with my own team. I have been praying for the sick and watching God heal people of every sickness and every disease for over 40 years. During that time I have often been surprised by how few believers have ever seen anyone healed and fewer still have ever seen someone healed as they prayed.

I have found that the primary concern that keeps Christians from praying for the sick is the fear of failure. "What if they are not healed?" It is not our responsibility to heal the person, it is God's responsibility and our responsibility to lay hands on the sick. When we are obedient, God is faithful. Christ is the Healer, we are the vessel He uses for His glory. Jesus has been given all authority on heaven and earth and the fullness of the spirit without measure. He is adequate for these things and our hope is completely in Him. His knowledge and power have no limits and His love has no end. If we do our job, He will certainly do His.

God's perfect will is for us to live in divine health. Why don't Christians live in divine health? This book will help open those reasons up to ALL believers so we can walk in divine health. Health was always intended by God to be normal for His children, "the children's bread" (Mt 15:26). God allowed His son to take stripes on His back for our healing because so many things came in to rob us of our health. Healing His children is His joy, healing the lost is His glory.

No sickness and no disease can stand against the power of God. We cannot allow ourselves to be paralyzed by the fear of failure when confronted by human suffering. If we allowed fear to stop us because of the reaction of men we would never share our faith with the lost. If we allow ourselves to be hindered in ministering to the sick by those who are not healed, we will rob many who would be healed of the freedom from suffering God wants them to have, and God the glory He deserves.

The church at large is blessed that God has raised up people like Randy Clark, Craig Miller and me who have persevered in the ministry of healing for most of their lives. In *Finding Victory When Healing Doesn't Happen: Breaking Through with Healing Prayer*, they have written a powerful book that affirms the love and healing power of God, while honestly facing up to the difficulties of human suffering.

In this book they share an abundance of testimonies illustrating both miraculous healings and those who were not healed with a wealth of insight into the root causes of sickness, while acknowledging the mysteries involved. This is a resource that contains the distilled wisdom of decades of ministering to the sick in many different parts of the world.

There are many books on healing, but this one should be considered mandatory reading for anyone who has battled getting their own healing and really desire to be used by God to heal the sick. Scripture tells us that those who believe will pray for the sick and they will recover! (Mk 16:18) Do not be intimidated by the task. Just as Jesus sent out the disciples, two by two, to heal the sick, so He will do with you (Lk 10:9). Jesus told them to heal the sick and to tell them: He is saying the same thing to His disciples today, because He does not change.

Study this book prayerfully and diligently. Learn all that you can from those who have dedicated their lives to healing the sick. Then, boldly pray for the sickness in your body, it has no legal right to be there. Look for areas that have not been given to God or past hurts that still affect you today.

Out of ALL the people in the world, HE has chosen you!!! He has chosen you, not to suffer like Jesus suffered, but realize Jesus suffered so we don't have to. God is going to give you opportunities to pray for the sick. He will open your eyes to those around you that need healing. He has positioned you right there to give Him glory. If you let Him, you will be astonished at all that He will do for you and through you.

JOAN HUNTER
Founder Joan Hunter Ministries
Author of Healing the Whole Man and Miracle Maintenance

INTRODUCTION

Have you ever prayed for someone who wants healing but nothing happens or they lose their healing after a short time? Have you ever had an emotional or physical condition and prayed, cried, and lamented for weeks or years with little change; only to give up trying or wondering if healing is for you or doubting your faith and becoming discouraged about what God is doing? These experiences can bring a mixed reaction of disappointment, confusion, doubt, and anger. Over time, your faith can be challenged to what you believe about healing. We are writing this book because we have been there too. We have been discouraged, frustrated, and have struggled with doubt. We have prayed for people who desperately wanted healing and the healing didn't happen. Then prayed for the next person, and they were healed. Although this makes us question why God chooses to answer prayers the way He does, we still want to seek more of God. We want more understanding of why some are healed and some are not and what is hindering our healing prayers. We thought it was time to look for answers and write down our experiences from a soul nature (mind, will, and emotions) rather than from a theological perspective. (For more information regarding the theology of healing one should read, *The Essential Guide to Healing*, by Bill Johnson and Randy Clark.) We want to emphasize that we do not have the answer, we believe we have partial knowledge, and trust others will add to this partial knowledge. We sense the truth of the Apostle Paul's statement from 1 Corinthians 13:12 "Now we see but a poor reflection as in a mirror; then we shall see face to face. Now I know in part; then I shall know fully, even as I am fully known." Before you get started, we want to pray Ephesians 1:18-19 over you. We pray that the eyes of your heart will be enlightened, so that you will know what is the hope of His calling, the riches of the glory of His inheritance, and the surpassing greatness of His power. . . May God pour His blessings over you as you read this book.

DR. RANDY CLARK & CRAIG MILLER

INTRODUCTION

PART ONE
HINDRANCES TO HEALING PRAYER

CHAPTER 1

PRAYER FOR HEALING

DR. RANDY CLARK

I once went to a Word of Faith Church, a small church, one that I felt I was called to. A woman came, who was not from that church, with a little boy, less than two years old. I found out that the woman was a single mother. Her husband left her when he found out that the boy was born with birth defects. The boy was blind, deaf, and missing most of his brain. He could neither communicate nor respond, and his mother was desperate for a miracle. I saved prayer for him for last, and I spent a lengthy amount of time praying, knowing he needed a miracle in creating his brain. The boy, to my knowledge, was not healed at that time, but there were many other healings that night. So many that later, an associate pastor told me that the faith in the people had become so high that people had gone to get their handicap children to bring to the night's meeting to be healed. I knew I should be thrilled, but I felt stressed. I went to the meeting that night, and there was the severely handicap boy that I prayed for. He was not healed. He is still alive, but he was not healed from his disease, and I felt so disappointed.[1]

Have you ever prayed for someone's healing and either nothing happened or there was only a slight improvement? After you get the courage to initiate praying for someone's healing, you can lose whatever courage you have left if little changes after you pray. What makes it worse is when you compare yourself with those *anointed healers* where everyone seems to get healed. The truth is, everyone has experienced prayers that have not manifested healing. You do not read much about the unsuccessful healing stories because they are not very encouraging, and people typically do not know what to do when healing does not happen. I believe it is important that everyone learn how to pray for the sick and what to do when there are little or no changes after you pray. It is important that you not compare yourself to others but rather focus on your own journey with God and what He can do through you. Every follower through Jesus has the ability to heal. You simply need to learn more about what you are able to do through the mighty healing power of God.

The importance of healing prayer

Healing the sick was central to the ministry of Jesus. In Matthew 4:23 it states, "Now Jesus went about all Galilee, teaching in their synagogues, preaching the gospel of the kingdom and healing all kinds of sickness and all kinds of disease among the people." Jesus left the assignment of healing the sick to his disciples, and the seventy, and to us through the Great Commission. Mark 16:15-18 reads, "And He said to them, 'Go into all the world and preach the gospel to every creature. He who believes is baptized will be saved; but he who does not believe will be condemned. And

---

[1] This story is an excerpt from Randy Clark, *The Thrill of Victory, The Agony of Defeat* (Mechanicsburg, PA: Global Awakening, 2009).

these signs will follow those who believe: In My name they will cast out demons; they will speak with new tongues; they will take up serpents; and if they drink anything deadly, it will by no means hurt them; they will lay hands on the sick, and they will recover.'" (NKJV)

Through scripture it is obvious that Jesus' ministry focused on healing the sick, but does that mean the sick can still be healed today? When reading the Great Commission, it seems clear to me that the answer to that is "Yes!" We are to do what Jesus did and commanded, heal the sick and cast out demons. This is commissioned for us now, today.

When does healing happen? Sometimes, healing can follow prayer, or it can come spontaneously during worship and praise. Other times, healing comes following a word of knowledge, which is a "supernatural revelation of information received through the Holy Spirit."[2] You may wonder how you can go about praying for someone's healing. Prayer teams that attend Global Awakening events and crusades use a Five-Step model (See Appendix), which includes an initial interview, prayer selection, prayer ministry, a re-interview, and post prayer suggestions.[3] You must check in with the person you are praying for to see if there is any improvement. For some conditions, they may not know right away, but for others they may know instantly if they are healed.

Does healing always happen?

I travel extensively, throughout the world, and I have met many people who used to pray for the sick, but they no longer do so. The reason they have stopped is because they have experienced what they believe to be failure. They have prayed for people who were *not* healed. Stepping out in faith and praying for healing means that you will see great victories and healings, but you will also see defeats.[4]

[2] For more information see: Randy Clark, *School of Healing and Impartation Revival Phenomena and Healing Workbook* (Mechanicsburg, PA: Global Awakening, 2009).

[3] Ibid.

[4] For more information see: Clark, *The Thrill of Victory, The Agony of Defeat.*

When you decide to pray for the healing of the sick, you must also decide and consciously choose to accept that you will not know all the answers. In fact, many times, you will have to admit you do not know why someone was healed and another person was not, why one person died and another received a miraculous healing. Not having all the answers makes us uncomfortable. The unknown makes us uncomfortable. But, if you want to see the sick get healed, you have to get comfortable with being uncomfortable.

Does healing always happen? The simple answer is "no." The more complicated answer is that healing does not always happen instantaneously and completely. For example, someone may experience 50 percent healing at the time of prayer and report three days later that they are healed 100 percent. Other people may walk away from you reporting no change in their affliction, but you should not lose faith for their complete healing!

All of us have people we pray for who don't get healed. There is such a mystery to healing ministry, but it is important to understand how much a healing ministry will cost.[5] Healing is in the cross of Luke 9:23, which reads, "Then he said to them all: 'If anyone would come after me, he must deny himself and take up his cross daily and follow me.'" This is the cross that bears healing. This cross associates with not victory, but suffering. The life of discipleship must involve suffering. Suffering is not of sickness and disease but rather of persecution, tribulation, and emotional pain for your faith.

Christian healing is a major area of suffering. As I mentioned, many people do not pray for healing. Some do not believe that it happens and have been taught to believe that it is not normative. Others, like Charismatics and Pentecostals, who do believe in healing, still do not pray for healing on a regular basis because they do not have answers. Answers like, why does one person get healed and not another? People want to succeed, they want to do well. They do not like experiencing disappointment.

[5] Clark, *The Thrill of Victory, The Agony of Defeat.*

People like to do what they are good at, and the problem with healing ministry is that you never feel like you are good at it.

If you are not ready to take up emotional pain, you are not ready to pray for the sick. It will hurt you when people do not get healed, but this pain is a cross we must bear if we are going to pray for the sick. You will have times that you see great victories followed by great acts of defeat, as though you are being tested, but faith is continuing and not giving up.

Stories of those not healed[6]

As I mentioned, I once attended a Word of Faith Church, where I experienced disappointment witnessing those unhealed. At the end of the conference, I taught on healing, and as I finished my message, a gurney came in with a sixteen-year-old boy on it who had massive brain damage. They rolled him in, and he was flailing on the gurney and was calling out. The parents had so much faith that they brought him to the front. They looked at me, and I felt the weight of their hope and faith, but he was not healed either. Hundreds of people that week were healed, but I cannot recall all of them. This boy and the aforementioned boy were not healed, and I do recall them.

I always pray for people in wheelchairs last so I can spend a lot of time with them and focus in on the prayer. I prayed once for a boy in a wheelchair who had spina bifida. I prayed for about twenty minutes, and he did not get healed. He said, maybe we should try praying for my sister instead, so we went to her. She was also in a wheelchair with cerebral palsy. Their parents adopted special needs children. So we prayed for the sister. She said she wanted to try to walk. All the way across the stage and back she tried to walk then collapsed in the wheelchair, not healed. Again, hundreds were healed that week, but these two stories I remember.

---

[6] These stories are adapted from those printed in Clark, *The Thrill of Victory, The Agony of Defeat.*

Another time, in North Carolina, three teenage girls ran to the altar after I spoke on healing. One of the girls was blind. She had sight until age seven, and then she started going blind. My heart was drawn to her, and I was sure she would get healed. Her faith was so strong. I prayed for her all week, and the last session, I asked if she could see, but she could not. When she did not get healed, I felt I had to tell her I was sorry that she had not been healed. The girl ended up writing me a letter that Christmas, and she told me to never stop praying for the sick. She actually ended up having a rare brain disease, and she later died. Her, I cannot forget.

A final story occurred when I was at an Evangelical church with a very small team. The first night I spoke of someone healed of Parkinson's disease. The second evening, a young girl, twelve years old, was leaning on her father as she could no longer stand on her own much anymore. She can tell that healing is not going to happen, and she starts to cry, and her nose starts to run, but she cannot get her arm to wipe it. I prayed so much for her that night. She was not healed. This disappointment, this is what happens between the great victories.

How to carry on when healing does not happen

When people do not get healed, you cannot give up. Giving up is letting the enemy attack. Giving up is moving backwards. Others can and will get healed, and we must carry on deeper. It is easier not to get involved in healing, but it is not right. I love when God refreshes us, but we cannot be shallow. We cannot stop praying because we cannot handle defeat. To carry this cross makes us more of a disciple of Jesus than those who do not. The gift of healing is not to bless us, but it is to bless others.

Chapter 2
What Hinders Healing Prayers

CRAIG MILLER

I was in the Brasilia, Brazil airport sitting at a table in the cafeteria area with some prayer team friends. We were waiting to fly home after finishing eight days of ministry with Randy Clark and a Global Awakening healing ministry team. As we shared about the week of miracles, one of my new friends named Mary mentioned about the pain she had in her knees for the past seven years. She explained that the cartilage had deteriorated to the point that bone rubbed on bone making walking extremely painful. I asked, "On a scale of 0 to 10 (10 being the highest pain), how much do your knees hurt?"

Mary replied without hesitation, "A twenty!" I was saddened and confused at the same time to hear her story. What I tried to understand was how Mary, a Godly woman of faith and active in a prayer ministry, still waited for healing for her own knees after years of receiving prayers from many others. So here we were finishing a week of healing ministry witnessing some of the most amazing miracles and Mary is on her way home with knee pain that she has had for years! That did not make any sense to me (and it never does). Compassion came over me with a strong desire not to let this trip end without her receiving what God did for all the others that were healed during this trip. Since I did not want to let the potential of another miracle fade away, I stepped out in faith by asking what happened seven years ago—when the pain had originated.

"That's when my husband and I sold our business and had to let go of all the visions we had for the future," she replied with a sad voice. As Mary shared her story of disappointment, the word, *failure*, came to my mind. I knew that word was from the Holy Spirit so I asked if the word *failure* meant anything to her.

She replied, "Yes, that is kind of how I felt," as I saw a tear fall down her cheek. Knowing you can move a mountain of hurt with just one tear, I realized something was releasing in her heart. So I pressed forward for more healing by asking, "Was there somebody you need to forgive?" She said, "Yes," and I led her to forgive that person so she could receive her healing. As she let go of old emotion, shame, and unforgiveness I saw her facial expression soften and her body relax. After I prayed to God for physical healing, I asked for her pain level. Her face lit up with amazement as she said, "A two!" I told her to walk around the cafeteria area praising God as she walked. When she returned I asked, "What's going on with your knees now?" With a smile a mile wide she started jumping up and down saying, "I can do this now. In seven years I have never been able to do this. And there's this squishy feeling growing in my knees!" At that moment she felt new cartilage growing! Praise God!

Now getting back to the subject of this chapter, the big question is, why was Mary not healed after years of people praying for her and then she suddenly became healed after a seven minute conversation? It's not that I have any special powers or abilities greater than anyone else. I just happen to believe that prayers can be hindered by how you think, believe, and deal with your physical and emotional conditions. I also believe that if God loves you and His son, Jesus Christ, died for your infirmities and diseases (Matthew 8:17), and the Bible scripture, "And all things you ask in prayer, believing, you will receive" (Matthew 21:22) is true, there must be something hindering healing from manifesting if healing doesn't happen after you pray. Like Mary, many people continue to live with a condition after years of prayer, medical treatments, and waiting for God to do something because you do not know what else to do. Over time you struggle to hold on to any hope for prayer to help while you wonder if God wants you healed.

Believe God is still in control

Even when you do not see or feel a change and you do not understand what is happening, you need to continue believing God is still in control. However, that can often be the starting point of your struggle. When you think and act out of the natural realm using your five senses, the healing process rarely makes sense. This is because God exists in the unseen spiritual realm which requires you to use faith (2 Corinthians 2:18) rather than the natural realm which makes you depend on logic by experiencing it before you believe it. Similar to when your child was very young and your child would totally trust you to stop the hurt from a skinned knee; you should have the same total trust in your heavenly Father who wants to heal you even more. If you do not have that kind of trust it is usually an issue of a hardened heart and a mind conformed to the world which hinders your ability to trust and step out in faith.

As a loving Father, God does not allow mind and body conditions just to keep you suffering- that would not be very loving and be considered abuse in some cases. Whether a condition exists because of a fallen world (sin), conditions that you consciously or unconsciously allow, or circumstances beyond your control, God still loves you and wants you healed. God wants you to have a healthy life according to the abundance He has for you (Ephesians 3:20). The purpose of this chapter is to learn about some of those reasons why healing is not happening and teach you how to identify what is hindering healing and effectively utilize strategies to bring healing to yourself and those you minister with.

Hindrances to healing prayer

When healing does not happen you want to determine which hindrance(s) may be affecting the healing process. Start by praying for the Holy Spirit to guide you into all truth and be sensitive to the words and behaviors of the person you are praying for (see Five-Step Prayer Model to learn how to pray for healing). If the healing does not happen after you pray, the following is a suggested guide to help identify a hindrance to healing and strategies to work through the hindrance.

Pray what to do next

When you pray to identify what is hindering your healing, be sensitive to hear what God has to say. Simply ask the Holy Spirit to reveal what is blocking the healing. Give yourself time to sense, listen, and believe the inward impressions or thoughts that come to you. What comes to your mind is often the answer you need. Remember God gives words that will build up, encourage, and comfort. Negative and hurtful words are not from God. If you struggle to hear from God, then you need to spend more time developing a closer, intimate relationship with God.

Watch and listen for clues

As you minister to others, observe body gestures and listen for words that reveal what the person is feeling, thinking, and believing. Over time, as you hear the various indicator statements found with each hindrance, you will get a sense of what hindrance may be affecting the healing. For example, if you hear self-condemning, judgmental, poor acceptance statements, it would suggest the person struggles with self-worth. If you see the prayee has their arms crossed that may suggest they struggle with letting you into their situation or they are holding in thoughts and feelings. If there is a chronic illness that does not seem to change, that may be an indication of suppressed emotional issues. As you read the following sections on hindrances to healing, you will become familiar with what may be hindering healing prayer.

SECTION 1:
UNWORTHINESS • UNBELIEF • FEAR AND DOUBT

Unworthiness

One common hindrance that is detrimental to healing is how you feel about yourself and what you expect to receive. When you do not feel worthy it is common to question, wonder, excuse, doubt, and just plain not expect good things for your life—especially healing. Although you can believe everyone else deserves healing, you do not feel worthy or good enough to receive good things in life and struggle to feel worthy of what God has for you. Unworthiness is usually created from your early life experiences and how you were treated by your early caregivers, primarily your mother and father. More specifically, the amount and type of loving affection and attention you received has a direct connection to whether or not you believe you are worthy to receive good things from God.

A woman came to see me for parent-child issues. When I asked about her own life she said she felt depressed because of chronic pain. When I asked for more details she told me about her lifelong scoliosis, two neck spurs, two lumbar bulging discs, and a pinched nerve in the sacral area of her back. In addition, she had a torn ligament from an auto accident that caused the left wrist to freeze, and the fingers, hand, and wrist to develop arthritis. She had been diagnosed with fibromyalgia and was unable to sleep from restless legs syndrome. She was daily taking three powerful pain medications. One pain medication, Valium®, was 500mg twice per day. After I explained about healing I prayed for God's healing several different ways. When there was no change in her sadness and pain, I sensed she was not receptive to my prayers, so I asked if she believed in her healing. After a moment of thought she said, "Yes, unless God wants it to be the thorn in my flesh." This statement confirmed she was still struggling with receiving her healing. As a result, I decided to dig deeper and asked if there was another time in her life where she felt pain from hurt she had received from others. In tears she shared about her abuse in childhood. After I helped her release the emotion from the past trauma, I told her about our heavenly Father loving her and wanting her to be healed. She forgave the people in her past and forgave herself for not believing healing was for her. I prayed again for God to bring healing, and a warm sensation came into her back and neck. The pain totally disappeared and she walked out pain free. Praise God!

How others treat you is the beginning of what you believe about yourself. If the important people in your life do not give you attention and are emotionally or physically hurtful, you will believe there is something wrong with you and feel unworthy to receive healing. The good news is you have a choice to either believe out of how the world treated you or believe what God wants for you to have as a child of the King. The truth is you are considered worthy of God's love (Matthew 10:30-31) and God wants you to know how worthy and good enough you are. You are *wonderfully made* in God's image (Psalm 139:14) and He loves you so much that He gave up His son, Jesus, to die on the cross (John 3:16) so your old nature can pass away and you can be made *new* (2 Corinthians 5:17).

Indicator statements

When there is unworthiness in your life, you will usually hear some form of self-condemning, judgmental, critical, and excusing statements that question the acceptance for healing. You may hear statements such as:

How can God love someone like me?
Maybe the healing is not for me.
I'm not good enough to be healed.

I've done too many bad things to be healed.

God may want this to be my thorn in my flesh.

Paul (in the Bible) didn't get healed, why should I?

Maybe I'm just supposed to suffer for God's sake.

Why would God want to love me or heal me?

I don't know if healing is God's will for me.

I don't know if I'm worthy to be healed.

Strategies to break hindrances to healing

You may ask questions such as:

- What has happened or who has hurt you to where you do not feel worthy to receive a free gift from God?

- Would you be willing to describe that hurt in order to release it to God?

- What has happened or who has hurt you to where you are willing to continue to live with this condition?

- If there was a way to change your condition would you allow God to give a free gift to make it happen?

- Describe the past situations that contributed to you believing this way.

  (Encourage the prayee to release their emotion and ask for forgiveness using the Heart Transformation for Emotional Healing technique—see Pages 95-98)

- If the prayee has a sense of unworthiness about most (or all) areas of their life, make a recommendation to seek Christian counseling to identify and release unresolved emotion and past traumas.

Unbelief (Lack of faith)

Unbelief can hinder what God would like to give and is directly related to what you do with the potential miracle waiting to happen for both the prayer minister and the one receiving healing prayer. Unbelief is often the result of circumstances involving injustice, disappointment, poor teaching, or misinformation. The more you are told healing is not for to-day the less likely you will believe healing will happen. The largest culprit of unbelief is usually unresolved hurt and distrust from others. The more you have been disappointed or hurt, the more likely you will not trust people and not believe their intentions or words. The earlier in life you have been hurt or disappointed, the more you will struggle to believe in others.

There was a man who had herniated discs in his back after lifting a large, heavy object. Over the next six months his back and leg muscles became weak with severe pain when he walked. After praying for God to bring healing on two separate occasions there was little change in his pain. During a third time of praying a week later I asked if he believed in his healing. He said, "I don't know if I'm supposed to be healed." I knew he had distrust of others as a result of childhood mistreatment by his father. I asked if he believed God loved him and that God wanted to heal him as any father would want for their child. Then he said, "Yes," I asked him to ask for forgiveness for his unbelief. I then placed my hand on his back and prayed for God's healing. I kept my hand on his back for ten minutes as we talked about God loving him while we thanked God for His healing. I asked what he felt and he said he began to feel tingling and warmth, with no pain. I kept my hand on his back until I sensed it was time to let go. I asked him to exercise his faith by standing and believing in his healing. He stood up and walked with no pain. Praise God!

Unbelief within the prayer minister, prayee, or someone in the room while you are praying may hinder the outcome of healing. In the story about the demon possessed boy, in Mark 9: 20-24, the father asked Jesus,

"But if You can do anything, take pity on us and help us!" Sensing the unbelief, Jesus questioned the father to change his thinking when He exclaimed, "If You can? All things are possible to him who believes." Realizing his mistake and unbelief the father immediately cried out and said, "I do believe; help my unbelief." After hearing the father's change of heart, in verse 25, Jesus delivered the boy of the unclean spirit. Anyone struggling with their belief about healing is not alone. Other Biblical examples where unbelief was involved are: unbelief of the religious people (John 12:37); unbelief in Jesus' home town (Mark 6:5-7); and the disciple's lack of faith (Mark 13:15).

Indicator statements

People with unbelief usually do not believe they deserve to be healed and struggle with believing what God can do for them. You often make excuses, rationalizations, and discouraging statements about God not healing to sidestep the personal responsibility or failure if the healing does not happen. These statements are also used to either excuse what you do not expect to happen or for self-protection to soften the disappointment if healing does not happen. You may hear statements such as:

I don't know if healing is for me.

If God want me healed, I would be healed by now.

Paul in the Bible didn't get healed, so it must not be for me.

Paul's Thorn in the Flesh means not everyone will get healed.

I don't believe healing will happen.

I'm going to have surgery in a month anyway.

You don't need to pray, I'm used to it.

Healing is not for today.

Strategies to break hindrances to healing

While unbelief indicates the prayee is struggling with loss, disappointment, rejection, and other emotional wounds of the heart it is important to identify and release those hurts in order for healing to take place and to remain in place.

Since unbelief can be a result of distrust caused from past hurt you may want to ask:

- What has happened or who has hurt you to where you are willing to continue living with this condition?

- If there was a way to change your condition would you allow it to happen?

- Describe the past situations that contributed to your believing this way.

  (Encourage the prayee to release their emotion and ask for forgiveness using the Heart Transformation for Emotional Healing technique—See Pages 95-98)

- If the prayee has unbelief throughout most areas of their life, make a recommendation to seek Christian counseling to identify and release unresolved emotion and past traumas.

Fear and Doubt

Fear is the destroyer of faith and doubt is the slayer of the potential for any belief you may have for something to happen. Fear and doubt often originate out of a wounded heart as a result of rejection, lack of love, unresolved loss, and various emotional or physical traumas. When there is a history of disappointment and fear from circumstances or people, you will continue to interpret life with fear and you will doubt the healing that God has for your life. You typically doubt or become afraid that your healing will not happen or fear your situation will become worse. Jesus tells us in Mark 11:23 if we do not doubt and believe it in our heart, what we ask for will happen. It is in the confidence and reassurance in what we believe without seeing or feeling is where our fear and doubt is overcome (Hebrews 11:1).

I was speaking to a friend who wanted prayer for arthritis in the knuckle joint that connected her thumb to her hand. For three years she had excruciating pain that required quarterly Cortisone shots to ease the pain. As a result of the arthritis, the thumb was frozen in place with little function. My conversation was definitely a God-incidence since she was planning to have extensive surgery the next day to replace the knuckle and cut the web between the thumb and index finger to provide movement to the thumb. I told her to put her other hand over the thumb as I prayed for God to bring pain relief and healing. When I asked her to take away her hand and begin moving her thumb, she said, "I'm afraid to take my hand away!" To encourage her I immediately took my authority in Jesus over the spirit of fear and told it to leave. Realizing that was a hindrance I prayed again for healing. This time she was confident to open her hand and move her thumb. The pain was gone and she was more encouraged to see what God could do. When we prayed for God to give more movement to her thumb, she began to move her thumb back and forth. Praise God! What was even more interesting is that God performed this miracle while we talked over the telephone! (P.S., when my friend went into the hospital for her scheduled surgery, she told the doctor about the miracle. The doctor simply said, "I've heard about things like this," and the surgery was cancelled.)

Indicator statements

Since fear and doubt are closely tied together it is important to listen to the words and watch the behaviors of the prayee when you talk about healing. Hearing the word "fear," negative statements, hesitation, apprehension, or doubt often indicates there are unresolved fears from past hurtful and fearful situations or disappointment. You may hear statements such as:

I don't think this is going to work.

I'm afraid I won't be healed.

What if God doesn't heal me?

What if God is mad at me?

I'm not ready for this.

I don't think I can do this.

I'm afraid to move too fast.

What if I'm not healed?

I'm afraid to try.

Strategies to break hindrances to healing

While doubt often indicates the prayee is struggling with more indirect wounds of loss, disappointment, rejection, and other emotional wounds of the heart it is important to identify and release former hurts for healing to take place and to remain in place. You may want to ask the following:

- What has happened or who has hurt you that you are willing to continue to live with this condition?

- If there was a way to change your condition would you allow it to happen?

- Describe the past situations that contributed to your believing this way.

  (Encourage the prayee to release their emotion and ask for forgiveness using the Heart Transformation for Emotional Healing technique – See Pages 95-98)

If the prayee has a level of fear and doubt that interferes with their normal daily functioning, make a recommendation to seek Christian counseling to identify and release unresolved emotion and past traumas.

SECTION 2:
UNFORGIVENESS • SIN

Unforgiveness

Unforgiveness is one of the most important and yet most neglected hindrances to any healing of the heart, mind, and body. Research shows that unforgiveness correlates strongly with the development of psychiatric conditions, medical conditions, and emotional issues. The Bible warns us that unforgiveness is a foothold for evil forces to make our conditions feel worse (Ephesians 4:26-27, 1 Peter 5:8) and we read about the importance of forgiveness since God cannot forgive unless you forgive others (Mark 11:25).

The Christian community views the act of forgiveness as a spiritual action and a step of faith that we choose to take to obtain healing and restoration. While in comparison, the American Psychological Association defines forgiveness *as an action or a process that involves a change in emotion and attitude regarding an offender.* No matter how you view forgiveness, it is a choice and an action that is essential to healing. Without it, healing does not happen. The advantage as a Christian is the availability of Christ's power to do what we cannot do on our own.

In 1975, a man was hit by a drunk driver while riding on a motorcycle. His spine was "blown out," knocking out a disc, partially severing his leg, breaking eight ribs, and puncturing his lung. For thirty-eight years the man felt his prayers had gone unanswered. His suffering had continued with one leg an inch shorter and extremely poor mobility because of the severe back pain. When I asked what his pain level was between zero and ten, he said, "It's always a fifteen!" He explained that he had to stop taking pain medication because the years of being dependent on the medications had taken their toll on his body. After he was able to release emotion and forgive the driver who hit him, I prayed for God's healing as I held his legs. We both watched as the legs moved, becoming even in length with the back pain completely disappearing. Not only was he able to stand and walk, but he could also bend and touch his toes without pain! The release of emotion and act of forgiveness brought healing to this man that no other source of medical treatment, physical therapy, medication, or previous prayer could bring over the last thirty-eight years. Praise God!

Forgiven but not healed

When you are praying for physical healing people are often caught off guard when asked about unforgiveness in their life because they don't understand its connection to healing. There are two ways people can react as they seek forgiveness. To make this simple I will call them *Head Forgiveness* and *Heart Forgiveness*.

Head Forgiveness is where a person will say they want to forgive but their heart is not ready to release the offender or emotion that goes with the offense. This person can have all the right intention to forgive but all the wrong ability to make it happen. Often they will go through the steps of forgiveness but the emotion will not be released. However, in healing ministries there is often the expectation that *Forgiveness = Physical Healing*. This is not always correct. I often see people that were assisted by well-meaning Christian ministries that lead a person through forgiveness prayer which makes the prayee automatically assume everything should be healed and "right with my soul." But when their condition returns, the person may either feel like a failed Christian, their faith is not strong enough, or healing was not meant for them. When in reality they are forgiven by God and He still desires healing, but the prayee was simply not ready to let go of the emotion. This is usually the underlying reason for not releasing the offense or the offender, which consequently creates a mental and physical foundation for the condition to remain (this will be discussed in more detail later).

For example, when you are praying to identify what may be hindering the healing and the Holy Spirit brings up an incident from the past, the most common response is, "I've already forgiven that person so I don't need to deal with that issue." Even though the offender was forgiven, the fact that the incident or emotion continues to come to your mind or body indicates that you are still harboring unresolved emotional issues.

Heart Forgiveness is when you are ready to release the emotion and the offender from your life, which at that moment, literally frees your body, mind, and heart from the bondage of that offense or situation. When the bondage is broken off, the healing power of God can be received. In the case of physical healing, the equation looks more like this: *Forgiveness + Emotional Release = Physical Healing*. Unforgiveness and suppressed emotion can keep each other hostage to unhealthy thoughts, feelings, and behaviors. In other words, both must be released to allow physical healing to occur (the next chapters will address this in more detail).

A woman had intermittent pain in her neck and shoulders since an auto accident a year and a half earlier. She lost her job and had difficulty maintaining her duties as a mother because of the pain and subsequent depression. Things were not going well, and the prayers over the past year were not working. During a conference break the woman asked me to pray for her. As the speaker of the conference I only had about five minutes before I needed to resume. So when I prayed for God to heal her neck, nothing happened. I prayed a second and a third time with no results. When I decided to ask the Lord what was happening, He said in my spirit, "Ask about forgiveness." So I said "Is there anybody you need for forgive?" (I realized in my rush to pray, I had forgotten to ask about forgiveness the first time.) She said "Yes, my mother and the driver who hit me." As soon as she forgave both of them, she immediately started sobbing to release the suppressed hurt. When I prayed again for God to bring healing, a tingling feeling moved down her neck and shoulders as she experienced healing. Praise God!

Reasons why we cannot forgive

If the act of forgiveness is so important, it does not make sense why you would hold on to unforgiveness. However, when you are so wrapped up in some inner struggle (anger, hurt or injustice) you do not see how illogical or unhealthy it is to hold on to unforgiveness. The following are some reasons why you cannot forgive.

Cannot let go of the emotion—If the prayee has a large amount of resentment, hurt, and anger, it can become more difficult to forgive until that emotion is first released.

Protection from being hurt again—People feel unsafe when they have been hurt. It is often the case that hurt and anger can be viewed as a source of protection or shield in order not to be hurt again. Until the prayee can feel safe, it is difficult to release the emotion.

Way of life—This is usually when people have lived in homes where unforgiveness is role modeled as a way of life or they have lived with an unforgiving heart for most of their life.

Believe you must be friends with the offender—When people believe or have been told they must be friends, get along, or "love the offender because you are a Christian," the prayee may feel it is easier to simply not forgive than get along with the offender.

Unworthy to be forgiven or God would not forgive—When a person does not feel good enough as a person they usually do not feel worthy enough to be forgiven.

Want to strike back or get even—When the prayee has a significant amount of suppressed anger from injustice and hurt in their life (either from their past and/or from a current incident), revenge is often thought of as the only way to make it right.

Sign of weakness—letting go of emotion or *giving in* to someone, can be considered a sign of weakness, letting someone win, or being taken advantage of. This is often believed if you have experienced offenses over the years and/or if the important people in your life (primary care givers) told you that expressing emotions was a sign of weakness.

Indicators

When a person is not ready to forgive you may observe the prayee:

- Gives one of the reasons why they cannot forgive (from the list you just read)

- Will tell you they do not want to forgive yet

- Goes through forgiving steps but unable to let go of emotion (anger or hurt)

- Cannot stop talking about the incident, the offender, and/or how they, or the offense, made them feel

- Has an emotional response (tears, anger) as they talk about the offense or offender

- Does not want to talk about the situation details

Strategies to bring forgiveness with other people

Since the condition of the heart is based upon what you think (Proverbs 23:7), it is important to release what is on your heart by talking about the incident. As you explain the events and share your feelings, the more hurt will be released and the faster you will move closer to desiring *Heart Forgiveness.*

The following questions and statements can be used to open up about what is on your heart:

- Tell me what it is about the incident that makes you feel so strongly that you cannot let go?

If the prayee continues to talk about the event but still cannot forgive, that is the telltale sign you may want to ask more about: any other injustice from the event, emotion felt from the incident, or any past injustices or hurts similar to the current incident.

You can ask questions such as:

- Tell me more about what happened to you.

- Are there other events or people in your life that have made you feel the same way?

- How did it make you feel when that happened to you? (Repeat this question as they bring up new information about an incident)

You can also discuss the following topics to emphasize the importance of forgiveness.

- Unforgiveness hinders the mind and body from healing.

- Forgiveness is not a feeling—it is a choice.

- God commands us to forgive (Ephesians 4:32).

- Without forgiveness we will struggle to experience God's blessings (Luke 6:35-38; I John 1:9).

- Ask God to help in the forgiveness process (John 14:16).

- Choosing not to forgive equals choosing to live with hurt.

- Choosing not to forgive (and holding on to the hurt) allows the offender and offense to be in control and keeps you in the role of a victim rather than a victor.

- Forgiveness does not change the fact that the other person may be wrong.

- Choosing to forgive equals taking control and choosing to become healthier.

Prayers to be used when you are ready to forgive:

Dear Heavenly Father, thank you for my ability to come to you in prayer. I now forgive (the offender's name) for the offense of _____. I forgive myself for holding on to this offense. Forgive me Father in heaven for my unforgiveness and thank you for forgiving me. Father in heaven, thank you for covering (the offender's name) and myself with your blessings. In the name of Jesus I pray.

Strategies to bring forgiveness with self

One area of forgiveness that is often missed is forgiving yourself for what you have done or said. You may believe that the situation is resolved after you forgive the offender, while either neglecting or unconsciously struggling to forgive your part in the situation. This struggle is often from incorrect Bible interpretation, denominational doctrine, or personal beliefs of unworthiness. The truth is that Jesus Christ died on the cross for your sins. When Jesus died, your sins were washed away. If you make a mistake, you can freely ask and quickly receive forgiveness. Forgiving yourself is a healthy way to move forward because receiving personal forgiveness provides the following:

- Forgiveness from God

- Release from spiritual bondage

- Closure to the situation in order to move forward

- Opens your mind to learn what to do differently

- Reminder you are worthy and deserving of forgiveness

- Point of acceptance after releasing self from personal mistake

- Reminder that God loves you and wants the best for you

If you are not ready to forgive yourself, the following can be used to open up about what is on your heart:

• What is it about the incident that makes you unable to forgive yourself?

  If you continue to talk about the event but still cannot forgive, that is the telltale sign you may want to ask more about: any other injustice from the event, emotion felt from the incident, or any past injustices or hurts similar to the current incident. You can ask questions such as:

• Tell me more about what happened to you.

• What is it that you have done that is so great that God cannot forgive? (When you do not allow God to do something for you, you are placing yourself above God.)

• Would you still love (and forgive) your own child if they did something wrong? If yes, then why wouldn't God, who loves you even more, forgive you?

Prayers when you are ready to forgive yourself:

My Heavenly Father, I am choosing to let this hurt go and forgive myself for _____. Thank you for the opportunity to forgive myself and help me not to take it back. In the name of Jesus I pray.

Strategies to forgive God

When you cannot forgive God the following may be present:

• Unresolved parent issues

• Misinformation regarding forgiveness

• Shame-based issues

- Unresolved emotion of anger or guilt
- Being grudgingly obedient
- Serving God but remaining mistrustful of His promises
- Believing what God says, yet remaining disobedient to His commands

The following questions can be used to help open up about what is on your heart:

- Tell me what it is about the incident that makes you feel so strongly that you cannot let go?

It is important to work through the following:

- What happened that lead up to why they are angry at God
- What God did or did not do
- The emotion that comes with the event or situation
- Working through feelings of injustice in ways God is believed to be unjust
- Forgiveness of people that were hurtful in similar ways to how God is believed to be hurtful

Prayer to forgive God:

Dear Heavenly Father, thank you for my ability to come to you in prayer. Forgive me for having the feelings and beliefs of _____ against you and help me to let these feelings and beliefs go. Thank you for forgiving me and taking this from me. Help me not to take any of it back. In the name of Jesus I pray.

Lastly, if the prayee cannot forgive, make a recommendation to seek Christian counseling to release unresolved emotion and past hurtful events.

Sin

While you may think of sin as one of the most common hindrances to healing, sin can also be one of the easiest to be cleared. All we have to do is ask for forgiveness (Ephesians 1:7). Once you are forgiven, sin only remains a hindrance if you keep living and believing you are a sinner. Everyone's perception of sin and the ability to receive forgivenesss is very different and typically created from what you are taught by the primary people and experiences in your life. If you learned you are always a sinner until you prove yourself worthy to be forgiven, chances are you grew up in an environment where love and forgiveness were conditional and you had to earn your way to being good enough and deserving of forgiveness. For example, if you struggle with unworthiness and guilt, you will often struggle with feeling forgiven. The truth is you are already forgiven because Jesus already died for your sin. As a result, when you accept Jesus into your heart, you are not a sinner anymore, but rather a forgiven child of God (Hebrews 8:12). You may occasionally make mistakes, but Jesus also died that you can ask for forgiveness and immediately receive it (Mark 11:25). Jesus died on the cross to save you and not condemn you. As the man who was a criminal hanging on a cross next to Jesus was instantly forgiven just by asking, you will certainly be forgiven for your sins when you ask (Luke 23:39-43).

A woman injured her knee a year ago and felt pain when she walked. The doctors said she would never play basketball again, which was her favorite sport. The woman shared details that she injured the same knee playing high school sports many years ago. At the time of the injury her parents elected not to obtain any medical treatment for the knee. She told me of her resentment toward her parents because of their decision to not treat her knee in high school which increased the problems with her current injury. She realized the resentment was making her feel worse and she believed she was sinning against God for holding on to the resentment. After asking for forgiveness for the resentment, I prayed for God to bring healing to her knee. She stood up, walked, and jumped with no pain. Praise God!

Indicators that sin may be hindering healing

Indicators include, hearing about wrongful acts, thoughts contrary to the Word of God, statements about sinning or statements such as:

I don't know if God will forgive me.

Why would God want to forgive someone like me.

I don't deserve to be healed.

I don't feel like I deserve to be healed.

Strategies

- If you hear of wrongful acts or behaviors, ask the prayee:
  Have you asked for forgiveness for _____.

- If there is sin, simply ask for forgiveness from God. *God forgive me for _____.*

- If the prayee continues to verbalize indicator statements, chances are the person still believes they are a sinner and does not believe in their forgiveness. This is a sign of a bigger problem of unworthiness, unresolved emotion, and/or unforgiveness from earlier issues. You may need to repeatedly reassure them of their forgiveness if you hear statements that indicate a lack of belief in forgiveness. It may be helpful to say and write down some scriptures that will reassure them of their forgiveness.

- Ask the prayee to describe the past situations that contributed to believing this way.
  (Encourage the prayee to release their emotion and ask for forgiveness using the Heart Transformation for Emotional Healing technique – See Pages 95-98.)

- If the prayee cannot resolve sin issues in their life, make a recommendation to seek pastoral or Christian counseling to release unresolved issues and past hurtful events.

SECTION 3:
WORLDLY EXPECTATION • CURSES • SPIRITUAL WARFARE

Worldly Expectations and Perception

Your healing can also depend on the availability of medical resources in the country you live, the level of awareness, and the willingness to utilize those resources. Interestingly, each country, whether it is industrialized or third world, has both positive and negative aspects to how resources are used for receiving healing. The abundance of medical resources used for healing in industrialized nations are the same resources that overshadows the need for healing by the God who created your ability to heal. By contrast, in countries where there is a lack of available medical resources there is often a corresponding abundance of faith for healing. Regardless of the amount of resources available, we tend to be creatures of habit which keeps you thinking, behaving, and expecting the same pattern of living with the same healing outcomes. The following are some examples of how your worldly expectations can influence your healing.

When your condition becomes your comfort zone

The longer you live with a condition, the more afraid you are to change beyond your level of comfort and understanding. People who have lost something, such as the ability to walk, can hope to regain what they once had. While people who never had the ability (born without the ability), do not have an expectation to what they never had. It is easier to have faith for something you once had than to pray for healing of something you have never known. This principle is shown in the following examples.

At a conference some time ago, God highlighted a woman sitting in the front row who had a hearing difficulty. During a break I asked her to step over to the side of the conference room where I found out she had lost 50 percent of her hearing in a boating accident fourteen years earlier and was eager for healing prayer. After I prayed for her healing God miraculously restored her hearing she said she could hear people talking from outside the conference room doors, on the opposite side of the room! Praise God! At another conference a few weeks later, I approached a woman who was born with 50 percent loss of hearing. Initially she was hesitant about receiving prayer but finally agreed after I shared about God's healing power. After I prayed for healing in the name of Jesus four different times with no change, she quickly rationalized the lack of healing by saying, "I've always lived this way, I'm used to it." Before I left I encouraged her to believe in what we prayed for to allow God to work in her life.

When your condition becomes your identity

The longer you live with a particular condition, the greater potential for that condition to define who you are and how you will relate with others. In the book, *Why People Don't Heal*, Carolyn Myss uses the phrase, *woundology* where she states the longer you are wounded the more it becomes your identity and the more you become dependent on the condition as a *secondary gain*. A secondary gain is where the condition provides a greater benefit than what the person would have without the condition. These benefits will come in a variety of ways such as physical, financial, social, or emotional support, or attention. The more needy or severe the condition appears, the more important the condition will become and the less likely the secondary gain can be detected. Rarely does the person start out with the intent to use the condition as a secondary gain. Instead, as the benefits from the condition become more and more gratifying, the easier it is to remain in the condition.

There was a man who had limited mobility as a result of severe pain from a knee injury. Over several weekly prayer visits he would leave each prayer time with no pain. During the third visit, he walked into the room with a limp using a cane just as he had the previous times we met. Since I believe God's healing is more powerful than what I was observing, I inquired more about what was happening in his life. I found out that after the injury his wife had taken on all the responsibilities he once had. This created resentment with his wife because of the financial and marital problems. I asked if he liked fighting with his wife, the lack of finances, and losing his place as a help mate and husband. He said, "No." I then asked if he wanted to be healed to change all of that. When he agreed, I prayed specifically for God to bring the total restoration of his knee, prosperity of finances, his will to be healed, and encouragement for his family.

This man needed a transformation of his belief system because he was getting secondary gains from remaining sick. He had to see for himself how the benefits of becoming physically well would outweigh the benefits of his condition. It is often the case that people with secondary gains must have their belief system shaken to make a transformation. In situations where another person is enabling the secondary gain, such as the spouse, it is important that person become part of the transformation process in order to stop the enabling cycle. When I encouraged the wife to let go of trying to save her husband, she was able to release her own guilt issues that perpetuated her enabling behaviors. (P.S. The man was healed and returned to care for his family.) Praise God!

Misinformation and poor teaching

Since most Christians have lived under some form of religious doctrine and authority, there is always the potential of receiving misinformation and wrong teaching. For example, among the most common expressions that is misused and misinterpreted to justify, rationalize, excuse, and explain away any problem that comes along is the phrase *Paul's thorn in the flesh* from 2 Corinthians 12:7. Sadly, people continue to be deceived into believing that if God would not heal Paul, your own healing should not be expected and you are destined to live with your suffering. However, that does not make sense. If you would not want your own child to suffer, why would your heavenly Father, who loves you immensely more, want you to suffer? If you were expected to suffer, people should be lining up to be in the hospital! Sickness is not from God and suffering does not glorify God.

Healing is from God and He only wants the best for His children; and you are one of His children. In preparation to visit a church I called the pastor to inquire about my praying for physical healing with the congregation during the Sunday morning service. After a moment of silence the pastor said, "Physical healing is not always expected - like Paul's thorn in the flesh." Although I gave a brief Biblical explanation about the significance of healing prayer, the pastor said he did not believe it should be done in his church. It is so unfortunate that the misinterpretation of this sole Biblical passage can deny and mislead so many people into losing out on healing in their lives.

The expression *thorn in the flesh* that is used in both the Old and New Testaments was never intended and was never indicated as an illustration for sickness. For example, in Numbers 33:55, the thorns in your sides illustrates the inhabitants of Canaan, in Joshua 23:13, the thorn illustrates the heathen nations of the Canaanites, and in 2 Corinthians 12:7-9, the thorn was referred to as the messenger of Satan (or angel of the Devil). More specifically the thorn in Paul's flesh was not a thing or sickness, but rather a demonic messenger sent "to torment me," (or "to buffet me," in the King James Version. The word "buffet" means to strike repeatedly as waves would buffet the sea shore).

Many religious traditions, have taught that the thorn was a sickness from the use of words such as "weakness" and "infirmity" in 2 Corinthians 12:9 and 10. Although infirmity does mean sickness, it can also mean *any lack or inadequacy*. One example is in Romans 8:26 that says, "the Spirit also helps our weakness (or *infirmities* in KJV)," which means, *not knowing what to pray for*. Regardless, Paul asked the Lord to remove persecution from him, not sickness, and the Lord told him His grace was sufficient. God's grace and healing power is sufficient for whatever issue you are dealing with. You are the one that must believe in His sufficiency.

Simply asking the prayee if they have ever been taught that healing is not for today can reveal much of what the person believes. (Some believe that the miracle of physical healing stopped when the last disciple of Jesus died. This belief is called cessationism.) The more childhood authority figures conveyed their own prevailing belief, the greater you will be conditioned to live with that belief as an adult. While I was ministering to a man with carpel tunnel syndrome, there was little success toward the healing of his condition. While I touched his hand I was led to ask about his belief in healing. He said he was brought to Christ by his father when he was a child and trusted the father's repeated teaching that healing did not happen after Christ's death. He concluded by using *Paul's thorn* as a reference. Realizing that his belief system may be blocking his healing, I sat back in my chair and explained the truth about Paul's thorn. I also found out that his father was not very loving, so I told the man how much God loved him. With tears of relief in his eyes, we prayed to God regarding his condition one more time and he was healed. Praise God!

When God is last

Another worldly expectation is how the amount of available resources affects your perception or level of importance of healing prayer. It is often the case in countries where financial and medical resources are readily available there is often less need or dependence on God as a source for healing. Conversely, when less options are available for healing (less resources financially, medically, etc.), there is a greater dependence on something beyond your means and ability. When I was ministering in

Brazil it was surprising how effortless it was to pray and see the mighty healing power of God become so alive in the people we ministered with. When I commanded an illness to be healed in the name of Jesus, you could see the excitement on the people's face as they believed and felt God's healing take place. When you have fewer options or resources, you must believe in something greater than the little you have. The comparable difference in industrialized countries when multiple resources are readily available; medical treatment can be as simply as swiping a credit card. As a result, you have the ability to control your own health options which decreases the need for God.

I was with a prayer team who prayed for a man with a torn meniscus in his knee. As the man explained about the injury and his expected surgery in the next two weeks, I sensed there was more confidence in the upcoming surgery than the God of our prayers. As we prayed, the confirmation of what I sensed became clear when the man began verbalizing in his prayers, "Well Lord, whether I become healed by the knife or by you, either one will be okay with me." As soon as he said those words I sensed a shift in the prayer team, as if the need to rely on our faith was somehow turned off. As a result, someone simply concluded with a prayer of encouragement for him and the upcoming surgery. What comes out of our mouth is usually what we believe in our heart (Proverbs 23:7). The words of the man shifted the faith atmosphere which consequently altered the prayer response.

It is important to note that believing in the healing power of God does not negate the importance of the medical profession or any professionals providing care. As a healthcare professional myself, I believe it is very appropriate for you to seek the best and most advanced treatment methods known, which also includes the divine healing of God. You have the right to expect a variety of advanced methods of treatment since any clinically competent practitioner's first priority and professional duty is to provide and allow you to pursue the best methods of healing known for the condition set before them. Anything less is providing substandard care which only reflects on the professional and their inability to provide services appropriate for those trusting in their care. A healthcare professional is only as clinically effective as the resources, knowledge, and ability he or she possesses.

Indicator statements

You may hear the following indicators when the prayee is reacting more out of what the world can offer rather than trusting in what God can do:

I was born this way.

I'm used to living this way.

I've lived with this my whole life…

I don't want to disappoint my doctor if I don't have the surgery.

If prayer doesn't work, I can still have surgery.

The doctor said I only have this much time to live.

I don't know how to believe any other way.

I'm going to have surgery next month anyway.

I don't know how to live any other way.

The doctor said it will take more time to heal.

Strategies to break hindrances to healing

Dealing with a prayee who is thinking, believing, behaving, and expecting from a worldly perspective can be frustrating and even hopeless at times. To help you keep a Kingdom minded perspective, here are some suggestions:

• Change the atmosphere with testimonies of what God has done.

• Keep your thoughts on what the Father is doing (John 5:19).

- Do not be influenced by any negative words or actions (Romans 12:2).

- When you pray ask the prayee to keep silent and just receive the prayer.

- Verbalize your excitement and encouragement with ANY changes you observe.

- Give frequent words of affirmation about how the Lord loves them.

- Believe God is healing, no matter what happens.

- Give scriptures to encourage the prayee—e.g., John 3:16, Matt. 8:17.

Ask the following questions:

- What has happened or who has hurt you that you are willing to continue to live with this condition?

- If there was a way to change your condition would you allow it to happen?

- Describe the past situations that contributed to your believing this way. (Encourage the prayee to release their emotion and ask for forgiveness using the Heart Transformation for Emotional Healing technique—— See Pages 95-98)

Curses

Since curses are not talked about much in churches, people typically either do not believe curses exist, lack knowledge of their existence, or do not believe they are a problem. In his book, *Blessings and Curses*, Derek Prince, states *a curse is an invisible barrier to receiving the blessings of a Christian life.*[7] Curses can come in the form of hurtful words and behaviors that are spoken over you or spoken by others which negatively affect your life. Although most people think of curses as magical spells that

---

[7] For more information see: Derek Prince, *Blessings and Curses* (Grand Rapids, MI: Chosen Books, 2003), 8.

negatively affect you, curses more often come in the form of destructive and critical words that you hear or say every day. This may include phrases you say to yourself such as, "What I did was so stupid" or "That was dumb." Or statements from parents or authority figures such as, "You will never amount to anything," "You're no better than your sister," or "God's going to be mad at you for that." Both *spells* and every day destructive words have a way of transferring to future generations through beliefs and negative words that are spoken by authority figures. The younger you are and the more often you hear these negative statements the more likely you will store them in your heart and become your belief system. Proverbs 23:7 states, "For what he thinks within himself, so he is." Even one negative statement believed in the heart can block prayers from getting through. Proverbs 12:18 of the NIV says "Reckless words pierce like a sword."

There was a man who had said his sight was quickly getting worse. We prayed for him but nothing seemed to happen at that time. I called the man a week later and asked how he was doing. He said there was no change. I was lead to ask if anybody ever said anything over him regarding his eyes. He thought about it and told a story about when he was ten years old, he and his mother were walking down the street, and there was a street beggar holding out a cup for money. The mom stopped to give some money, the street beggar pointed to the boy and said "Young man, you are going to be blind like me one day." He did not like that experience but did not think much about it since then. I took my authority in the name of Jesus and we cut off that curse. As I prayed a second time for God's healing touch the man stated he instantly felt something lifting and coming out of him. Praise God!

Curses can also come in the form of medical conditions or spirits transferred to people and even animals. A woman requested prayer for pain that started in her left rib cage and radiated down her hip to her left foot. She could not walk from excruciating pain. As we explored all possible origins of the pain, she mentioned she was a counselor and remembered counseling with a family where she felt a "dark" presence that filled the room. The pain in her left side started that same evening for no reason. Struggling to move with the pain, she wanted her Golden Retriever to move out of the way so she could walk to the kitchen. So, she very gently touched the dog's left hind leg with her own left foot. When the dog got up to move, the dog immediately started severely limping on the left side. The dog was taken to the vet with an x-ray showing a dislocated left hip with the left hip bone hanging one inch below the socket. The doctor recommended surgery to fix the dislocation. When I prayed for God to bind any curses, she felt something immediately release from her. As I prayed for God to heal her body, the legs and arms became even in length, the pelvic bone came into alignment, and her pain totally disappeared. After the woman asked God to bind any curses that were transferred to the dog, she very gently touched her dog on the left hind leg with her healed left foot. In less than five minutes the dog's left hind leg immediately went back into place and started walking perfectly straight with no limp or pain. Praise God!

Indicator statements

There may be a sense of gloom in your heart or feeling like a dark cloud is following you. You may hear self-cursing statements such as:

I'm such a failure.

I'm so stupid, clumsy, going to fail, unworthy, dumb…

I promised myself I'd never be like my mother.

That was stupid; I don't know why I did that

My mother had the same condition.

I inherited this from my father.

My mother said I wasn't planned to be born.

I was told I'm: crazy, ugly, stupid…

I have asthma (or any condition).

The doctor said I have…

Strategies to break hindrances to healing

If the prayee has multiple experiences of word or behavior curses, pray to release the curses:

In the name of Jesus Christ of Nazareth, I declare the blood of Jesus to bind and cast away every curse and hurt that has and could ever come upon me from those in my life now and the generation before me. So I ask you now heavenly Father to release me from every curse, every evil or hurtful emotion over my life, in Jesus' name. By faith I now receive my release and receive my heavenly Father's blessings over my life. Thank you Jesus for my freedom and blessings.

Extra note: You do not need to memorize the above prayer. There is no one particular prayer formula to clearing curses and spirits from your life. What is important is that you take authority *in the name of Jesus* to bind and cast away what is evil and ask to release from heaven what is good and of God.

Spiritual Warfare

Spiritual warfare (or demonization) is less often talked about in religious settings and is often misinterpreted as a dysfunction of the mind and body, such as a physical or mental illness. In essence, spiritual warfare is when demons spiritually affect the mind and body in ways that would appear to be outside rational thought, actions, and body. Demons cannot totally take over the body and mind of a born again Christian but can influence, misguide, oppress, harm, and overwhelm the mind, body, and spirit.

Different religious circles view demons as either the direct cause of a mental or physical illness and/or as a way to inflict more torment on an illness that already exists. Regardless of how demons affect you, not all illness or disease is caused by demons (Mark 5 and Luke 6). The Bible differentiates between those physically sick and those demonized. For example, there are eighty references to demons (counting the repetitions) in the New Testament with eleven indicating a distinction between illness caused by demons and illness caused by sickness. A few examples are, Mark 1:32, "When evening came, after the sun had set, they began bringing to Him all who were ill and those who were demon-possessed," and Matt. 8:16, "When evening came, they brought to Him many who were demon-possessed; and He cast out the spirits with a word, and healed all who were ill." What is most important to remember, as a believer, is that you have the power and authority over the enemy (Mark 16:17). As a result, the enemy should be more afraid of you than you are of him. If not, then you need to be more in God's Word and build your personal relationship and understanding of God. Dr. Unger writes in his book, *What Demons do to Saints*, "A believer who centers his life in Christ causes the power of darkness to tremble."[8]

A man developed irregular heartbeats, pressure in his chest, numbness in his fingers, and severe pain in his shoulders that radiated down his arm. Thinking he was having a heart attack he went to the local hospital. After many tests, the doctors ruled out a heart attack but could not identify the origin of the problem or give any conclusive diagnosis. The symptoms subsided after a long night in the emergency room and was sent home with pain meds and a follow up doctor's appointment. A few days later, some of the symptoms returned and have continued ever since. After discussing his

---

[8] For more information see: Merrill Unger, *What Demons Can do to Saints* (Chicago, IL: Moody Press, 1991), 19.

life the man shared about his sixty hours per week, tremendously stressful occupation and years of family turmoil. Acknowledging something felt wrong in his spirit, he agreed to go through deliverance. During this session the spirit of *torment* was very heavy and came out released with a great amount of tears and fear. Since the deliverance he reported no medical issues and has continued to claim his healing. Praise God!

Demonic spirits can enter into your life through personal activities, from people you associate with to generational issues that are transferred to you. For example, during your interview with the prayee, if you suspect spiritual warfare you should ask about personal or generational involvement with: occult, Free Masonry, Ouija boards, séances, talking with the dead, palm reading, satanic issues, ritual abuse, sorcery, witchcraft, family history of depression, oppression, suicide, financial poverty, medical or mental illness.

Indicators

The following are indicators (or manifestations) that may have been in your life for years or may suddenly appear just before, during, or after you pray with them. It is very important to note that these manifestations *do not always* suggest the involvement of demonization (influence of a demon), however, there is a strong possibility of demonization when the manifestations persist when all other avenues of healing have been unsuccessful.

Body indicators may include, shaking, hissing, vomiting, dry heaves, rocking and twisting, erratic and wild behavior, crying out, chronic feelings of numbing, heaviness, darkness, doom, gloom, smothered and overwhelmed with life, self-mutilation (repeated harm to self), rolling on the floor, and any behaviors outside rational actions.

Mind indicators may include long term or sudden cloudy, clutter, or chaotic thoughts, seeing dark shadows, delusional thoughts, thoughts of self or harm to others, hearing threats, self-harm or evil voices.

Strategies to break hindrances to healing

The key to responding to spiritual warfare is not struggling to know *everything* about the schemes of the Devil (although it is good to know some things) but rather having an intimate relationship with Jesus Christ. Spiritual warfare should not be a battle because the Devil has already been defeated. You are not the one dealing with the Devil anyway since that is the job of God and His staff. If you are uncomfortable with the thought of dealing with the enemy, that is confirmation your spiritual life is still about you and you would benefit from learning more about your power and authority in Jesus Christ. Jesus did not tell us about the one who came to kill, steal, and destroy (John 10:10) without giving us the authority to send evil away (Acts 1:8, Col. 2:9-11). Until you are ready to pray with someone that has demonic manifestations it may be best to refer the prayee to someone who is more knowledgeable with demonization.

The following are general suggestions for spiritual warfare

• Review the Global Awakening Prayer for Deliverance listed in the Appendix.

• Indicators (or spirit "manifestations") that suddenly appear during prayer time are a tactic of the enemy to scare you and divert your attention from delivering the evil spirit. I had a woman that began hissing and growling in a way that would scare anyone unaware of what was actually happening. As soon as I began to take authority in the name of Jesus the woman started having dry heaves as the evil spirits were releasing and the woman was freed.

Suggested prayer over prayee (or have prayee repeat prayer): *In the authority I have in Jesus name I command this spirit of ___ to be bound and sent away. I plead the blood of Jesus over (person's name) and bring peace into their mind and body. Thank You Jesus for Your protection.*

- When the prayee suddenly cannot remember or their mind is confused, blocked, dark, black, blank, or wandering, take authority against whatever you hear or see. When you ask questions and you hear statements like, "My mind went blank," or "I feel confused," in the name of Jesus take authority over the problem and send the spirit away.

Suggested prayer for prayee to repeat:

In the name of Jesus I command the spirit of <u>(what the prayee says)</u> to be bound and sent away. In Jesus name, I release from heaven the Spirit of <u>(the opposite)</u> and receive the blood of Jesus as my protection.

- If the prayer minister or prayee see or feel sudden darkness, fear, objects move, shadows, etc., ask Jesus to send away whatever you see or feel. While a woman was sharing about her life she suddenly stopped talking and with wide eyed concern on her face said, "Did you see that?" She continued, "It was a dark shadow that moved to the back of me." Even though I physically did not see the shadow, I sensed evil in the room (I will believe what the client says until proven otherwise). I simply took authority over the shadow by telling it to leave in the name of Jesus. We were not bothered by it again.

Suggested prayer for prayee to repeat:

In the name of Jesus I command the spirit of _____to be bound and sent away. In Jesus name, I release from heaven the Spirit of <u>(the opposite of what you sent away)</u> and receive the blood of Jesus as my protection.

Other suggestions:

- Do not get into a conversation or answer questions of the enemy. Always bind them and ask Jesus to send them away.

- If the prayee is not a born again Christian, lead the person to salvation before deliverance.

- If they were in occult or other demonic activity, have them renounce Satan.

- Encourage the person to take authority when they are on their own.

- Tell the prayee, *Jesus is in you, Jesus loves you, you are victorious.*

- Ask for protection by praying the blood of Jesus over yourself, the prayee, and their family.

- Use the Prayer of Deliverance listed in the Appendix.

- Refer the prayee to a pastor or Christian counselor if spiritual warfare persists.

Chapter 3
When Emotions Hinder Healing
CRAIG MILLER

Your emotions can be one of the most significant influences to hindering healing. The fact that the Center for Disease Control and Prevention reports 85 percent of all diseases have an emotional element, underscores that unresolved emotion plays a powerful part in the healing of mind and body conditions. In the book, *Your Child, Birth to Age 6*, Fitzhugh Dobson and Ann Alexander comment that the inability to express emotions is one of the basic causes of many neurotic problems and psychosomatic diseases [medical condition originating from the mind rather than the body]. "A child who has not learned how to express emotions will be severely handicapped as an adult."[9] This emphasizes the vital importance of expressing God's gift of emotions.

---

[9] For more information see: Drs. Fitzhugh Dobson and Ann Alexander, *Your Child, Birth to Age 6* (NY: Simon & Schuster, 1986), 250.

The knowledge that suppressed emotions impacts the mind and body has been around for centuries. As early as the 1930's, observations and writings by professionals such as psychiatrist Sigmund Freud noted how repressed emotions can turn into a mind or body condition. For example, the mind has the power to actually mimic a physical ailment as a way to protect your mind from the stress or emotion you cannot consciously deal with. There was a woman named Sarah who was hospitalized with left side paralysis, slurred speech, and other stroke-like symptoms. After a medical work-up the doctors were baffled because even though the laboratory tests and neurological evaluation could not confirm the stroke diagnosis, she still exhibited the symptoms for that condition. When I was called in to provide a psychological and social evaluation I reported that the symptoms began after Sarah became very depressed after a family crisis and her husband took time off from work to care for Sarah and the children. It was first believed the stroke symptoms were the result of the family trauma she experienced. Upon further evaluation, I found that Sarah and her husband did not have a healthy marriage relationship for some time, and Sarah was so deprived of love and attention that the stroke symptoms came about, not from the trauma of the family crisis, but rather as a psychosomatic condition to satisfy the "secondary gain" of keeping the husband at home to care for the family and receive his attention. Since there was no medical evidence to substantiate the stroke diagnosis, the medical team gave her a mental health diagnosis of *Conversion Reaction* [when an emotional state is converted into a physical state]. It was necessary for Sarah to address the emotional issues in order for the physical condition to be healed.

How emotions affect the mind/body conditions

When a trauma happens in your life there are a succession of changes to your mind, body, and spirit. You naturally react to that trauma through your five senses such as a physical feeling, unforgettable sight, and distinctive sound or smell. These sensations are registered in the brain to assess how the body and mind will handle the trauma. If part or all of the emotional or physical event is too traumatic to handle, the mind can shut off (or supress) the emotional and/or the physical part of the incident. The supression of memory is a natural reaction of the brain to assist the mind and body from becoming too overwhelmed by the physical incident or the emotional trauma form the incident. As a result, the supressed trauma can become permanent impressions in your body and mind that will never leave unless you someday release them. If the emotion from the trauma is not released it becomes held in flesh, cells, muscles, tendons, posture, organs, memories, and thoughts. The more your physical body absorbs the emotional energy the more physical symptoms are the result.

Through his literary research and private practice Dr. Dennis Cousino, a naturopathic physician, international speaker, and founder of Dynamic Health has stated that there is a growing body of evidence showing that every cell and all emotions have their own unique vibrational signature that resonates within your body. When we alter the flow of energy or change vibrational patterns, we can see evidence at the physical, mental, and emotional levels. Every cell has an emotional receptor site that receives the positive or negative vibrations from the external environment. If something happens which creates a negative emotion and that emotion is held inside, over time that negative vibrational signature will alter the cells throughout your body and mind to vibrate at the same level as the negative emotional vibration. For example, the vibrational patterns for the emotions of anger resonates similar to the vibrational patterns of the liver cells. Chronic anger will negatively affect the health of the liver by lowering its vibrational output to a less optimal level, which makes it more susceptible to disease. However, the reverse is also true. When you release the negative emotion and replace it with God's peace, love, and joy, the same vibrational emotion will be experienced by the body and mind. Consequently, your emotional and cellular vibrational patterns can greatly influence your destiny of health or sickness.

Body conditions—physical

The feelings that are pushed down (suppressed) will accumulate inside and fester like a disease that grows out of control. The suppression of feelings can create inner stress, which subsequently can hinder the body from fighting off disease and hinder the production of brain chemicals that elevate your mood to feel better. Similar to what Dr. Cousino previously suggested, if the emotions are not resolved the accumulation of suppressed hurts and stresses can eventually show up as physical conditions in the body. For example, overwhelming anxiety and long-term feelings of unjust treatment can cause stomach and digestive conditions. Long-term unresolved grief can cause lung conditions, unresolved issues of fear can cause kidney conditions, and unresolved anger and frustration can cause liver conditions (for more details see Suggested Emotional Connection to Body/Mind Conditions on page 143). The following are some specific examples of chronic body conditions that were healed by prayer after the corresponding suppressed emotion was released.

Allergies

As you suppress physical or emotional trauma, the mind will store the emotional and physical traumas in *unconscious memory* and in *body memory*. The body will create symptoms as a substitute to release what the mind cannot bear to deal with. For example, hay fever is a substitute for suppressed tears. In addition, present everyday circumstances can be triggers that release old trauma symptoms that become misdiagnosed as mental health or physical conditions. A man suffered with shortness of breath, light-headedness, and overwhelming feelings when he was around new carpet, new paint, new mattresses, or anything with strong chemical smells. He was diagnosed with allergies and treated for years with medication with little improvements. During treatment for other emotional issues, one particular event stood out where he was beaten so severely by a parent he vomited and urinated while lying on the floor. Since your mind will suppress the memory and emotion from the trauma as a way to protect yourself from becoming overwhelmed emotionally, the original emotions from the trauma were still part of his life. As a result, any strong smells triggered up the unresolved emotional from the past traumatic events. When the past emotion was released the physical symptoms he suffered for years that were mistakenly diagnosed as an allergy were eliminated. Praise God!

Arthritis

For ten years a woman was diagnosed with osteoporosis and arthritis. She had very limited mobility with severe pain in her lower back, legs, and feet with her toes deformed at a 45 degree angle. She was a woman of strong prayer and faith that could not get free from her suffering. When she told me she was diagnosed with osteoporosis ten years ago, I asked what happened at that time. She shared that her husband died, and there were other multiple traumas from abusive family members she had experienced through life. She admitted to feeling guilt, anger, resentment, bitterness, and sadness, which are some of the emotional origins for arthritis. I knew it was important to release the suppressed emotion before we prayed for her physical healing. After the woman released her emotion from the past traumas and forgave each family member for their specific abusive act, I prayed for God to bring physical healing. At that moment, 75 percent of her pain decreased. Each time she released emotion and forgiveness from other abusive situations, the physical pain quickly decreased until she was completely pain free. I then prayed four times for God to straighten her toes without seeing a change. She left with the pain totally gone but the toes remained deformed at a 45 degree angle. Three days later I spoke to her and she said the morning after the healing, she woke up and her toes had straightened out by 50 percent. Praise God!

Cancer

As with many ailments, unresolved emotion is a common theme and the condition of cancer is greatly influenced by life issues that are still lingering in your mind and body. A man who was diagnosed with prostate cancer was scheduled for surgery to remove the prostate. When he described having emotional feelings of anger with physical discomfort and restrictions in the mid-section of his body, he realized these were the same sensations felt during his childhood abuse. The more he remembered about the past trauma the more he realized the connection to what he felt as an adult. After he was able to release the emotions from the past issues and forgive those who hurt him, I prayed for Jesus to destroy the cancer cells and bring healing to his prostrate. A subsequent medical evaluation revealed his prostate condition had improved to such an extent that the surgery was cancelled. Praise God!

Chronic back pain

Since suppressed emotion often releases through the weakest physical part of the body, and it is suggested that 80 percent of Americans (85 percent worldwide) have some form of back problems and that chronic back pain is among the most common holding area for suppressed emotion. Since the spinal column functions as the major structural support for the body, it is not a coincidence that the major underlying emotional influence for chronic back pain is having little emotional support and being unable to cope with emotional difficulties.

A woman asked for prayers to heal the severe pain she had in her back for many years. She was a woman of strong faith and admitted that nothing seemed to make a permanent change in her condition. As a result she had difficulty walking, standing, and sitting without severe pain. After praying for Holy Spirit wisdom, she remembered hurting her back when she was violently pushed to the floor by a family member twenty-five years earlier. When I asked her to think and feel what happened during that time, she admitted to a sensation of fear and hurt that was still felt in her heart and body. She admitted to living with an emotionally unsupportive family members which she believed made her condition worse. When she released the emotions from the past and forgave the family members, I prayed for Jesus to heal her back. When she stood up and walked around the room she was pain free. Praise God!

Fibromyalgia

Among the origins of fibromyalgia is the accumulation of emotional pain from life hurts that transfers to physical pain in the muscles, ligaments, tendons and other soft fibrous tissues in the body. You emotionally and physically feel immobilized causing your life to feel shut down. The physical pain limits you from moving and becomes a distraction from dealing with deeper emotional issues. A woman asked for prayer who was diagnosed with fibromyalgia and arthritis for the past five years. Her pain was so severe that her movements were limited and simply taking a shower was very painful. As a result, she had to quit her occupation and live on disability. She revealed that her ex-husband was physically and emotionally abusive and had parents who were not emotionally supportive. As a result she suppressed her emotional pain, unforgiveness, and bitterness. Once she released the emotional pain from the past hurts and forgave her parents and ex-husband, I commanded in Jesus' name for the arthritis to leave, for oxygen to come into her blood, and to heal the joints, muscles, and tendons. Her body pain decreased by 75 percent. We praised God for what happened and continued to pray for more healing. I asked her to exercise her faith with walking as I repeated encouraging statements to her while we walked together. The more she walked the more her pain decreased and the more she became encouraged to expect more healing. When she was done walking she was completely free of pain and totally healed! Praise God!

Irritable Bowel Syndrome

At a conference there was a prayer team of four people praying for a woman that had terrible pain and discomfort from Irritable Bowel Syndrome (IBS) for the past twenty years. Since our initial prayers did not change her condition I asked for more details of her life. The woman denied any traumatic events as both parents were present and denied there were any issues out of the ordinary. At that point, I decided to explore deeper because I knew IBS was an emotionally based condition and the team had not pressed deep enough emotionally. When we were told the parents were "alcoholics" and "yellers," I knew I found my source of origin. When there is a condition that does not heal, one of the indications of deeper emotional issues is when the person denies having childhood issues. When you grow up in chaotic, unloving, abusive, and/or emotionally lacking homes children must normalize the conditions by suppressing and rationalizing the emotion to survive. The child grows up numb to dysfunctional situations creating the lie that everything is fine but continues to feel emotionally torn up inside. The emotion from *anxiety* and *unable to control or eliminate your circumstance* settles in the bowel area. This woman was so shut down emotionally, it took two different nights at the healing conference to help her release enough emotion for the pain to subside. As she released the hurtful emotion and forgave the people who hurt her, inner healing started and the IBS condition began to heal. Praise God!

Lung condition

Since the lungs sustain life with the air that creates the energy for all the systems in the body, any loss of functioning can be felt as a loss to your body to live life. Long term suppressed feelings of loss such as grief from losing someone or something can bring devestation that greatly affects your life and can settle in the lung area. Six years ago a man quit his job when his doctor stated the toxic fumes from the job was the reason for his severe decrease in breathing capacity. He could not walk distances or climb stairs without shortness of breath. For years he had prayed for healing with little results. Just after leaving his job, he went through a difficult divorce which created overwhelming grief that had never been released. This unresolved emotion had affected his physical state prior to the job loss. Aware that unresolved grief can affect the condition of the lungs, I assisted the man to release his grief from losing his family and job. When I prayed for God to heal his lungs, his air passages immediately opened and he was able to breathe better than he had in years. He has not had lungs problems since that time. Praise God!

Mind conditions—thought and behavior

Kenneth Pelletier, PhD. in his book, *Mind as Healer, Mind as Slayer*, comments that stressful experiences create certain methods of coping with your problems which become the routine for how you will handle that stress. When this high stress level is prolonged it produces a change in your mind to create the preconditions for a disorder.[10] The following are some examples of mind conditions that were healed after releasing the corresponding suppressed emotions.

Anxiety

Anxiety can be caused by a variety of issues such as environmental factors, medical factors, genetics, brain chemistry, or substance abuse. One of the most common is overwhelming stress from negative situations where you feel little control, especially from childhood. When you suppress the anxious feelings, it will accumulate to more overwhelming feelings later. For example, if you had fears as a child when your parents

---

[10] For more information see: Kenneth Pelletier, *Mind as Healer, Mind as Slayer* (New York, NY: Delta Book, 1977), 117.

yelled, you will suppress the emotion to get through life. Those suppressed fears will later be triggered by adulthood arguments as having a *fear of conflict*. When you feel anxiety at any age, it is always best to identify and heal the original cause of the anxiety; otherwise it will only become worse. A woman told me she had been anxious for sixteen years. When I asked what happen sixteen years ago, she said it was a very stressful time in her life with a miscarriage and subsequent nervous breakdown. Since she wanted to be healed of her anxiety, I asked her to share her story and feelings about the miscarriage. When she released the feelings of sadness and regret, she was able to forgive herself and the anxiety immediately left her. She felt totally renewed in her body and mind. Praise God!

Dissociative Identity Disorder
(formally known as multiple-personality)

When faced with trauma that is emotionally and physically overwhelming your mind will disassociate (separate) your emotional self from the physical self as a way to protect you from that situation. In severe situations of abuse your powerful mind can create other personalities (alters) to help you deal with the emotion of the situation. If the emotion from the trauma is not addressed and healed, the mind may continue to use the *alters* to help deal with stressful situations the rest of your life.

During a conference a woman who came to me for healing prayer, said she was sad and felt like she lived in chaos every day while she lived with fifteen identified alters. She believed the chaos and alter personalities were the result of the abuse she suffered during childhood. In prayer, I asked the Holy Spirit to take her back to when she first felt sadness and chaos. When she shared her childhood situation I prayed for Jesus to bring His healing power. The woman wrote the following personal testimony about her healing: "Inside, it was like an unruly classroom with no teacher. . . voices, arguments, uncontrolled emotion, empty and not belonging. Craig asked me to have Jesus show His love for me at the point where I first felt alone and unwanted, rejected, unloved . . . it was in utero, in my mother's womb. His peace and love filled me as I yielded to him. He [Jesus] held me and I was filled with His peace and love. I no longer felt alone. I belong to Jesus and He belongs to me. I don't need my alters anymore. They became part of my whole. I am restored to peace and victory for the first time in fifty years." Praise God!

Bipolar

Bipolar disorder is an illness believed to be caused from a chemical imbalance that can involve one or more episodes of serious mood swings from a "high" (euphoric) feeling and/or irritability to the opposite feeling of sad and hopeless (depression), with periods of a normal mood in between. The symptoms typically can begin in adolescence or early adulthood. Since these symptoms are treatable with medication, people may have a tendency to become more reluctant to rely on God for a permanent cure. Although it can become intimidating to pray for mental health issues, it is best to cast away in Jesus name what the prayee describes as the problems and proclaim healing by praying for God to heal the body with the opposite. For example, a man diagnosed with bipolar complained he felt "upside down," "not right inside his body," and "didn't feel right about life in general." I prayed for God to bind the spirit of bipolar and brain imbalance and for God to restore the polarity of his body, bring proper balance to his brain and body chemistry, and bring the spirit of joy in his life. As the man was leaving I also instructed him how to believe in his healing. Three days later he reported feeling totally changed inside and felt "right" ever since. Praise God!

Obsessive Compulsive Disorder (OCD)

Unresolved stresses and anxiety in your life can create behaviors to keep life in check and in control. The more you fear being out of control in life circumstances, the more rituals, thoughts, and repeated behaviors are needed to feel in control of life, which is just one potential explanation for the development of the condition called Obsessive Compulsive Disorder. The longer the emotion is not addressed from the original stressor(s), the more obsessive you will become to protect yourself from feeling out of control or that something bad will happen if life is not in order. A man had been obsessive about cleaning, checking, and worrying for years. Throughout his life he felt anticipatory anxiety about doing new things and a heavy or tense feeling in his chest. When I asked the Holy Spirit to take the man back to where he first felt these feelings, the man envisioned himself as a child with his strict, yelling father who was always demanding and correcting the boy. Subsequently, the father's hurtful treatment created the belief of not being good enough and an obsessive behavior from the fear of his father's wrath. When he shared his earliest hurtful memory, he was able to release his original fear and forgave his father. I then asked the Holy Spirit to reveal the truth that he was good enough, worthy of good things, and had peace of mind. The obsessive and compulsive behaviors and thoughts disappeared. Praise God!

Depression

Depression is a very common condition that affects the mind and body that can be due to heredity, chemical imbalance, living in depressed homes, and a natural response to loss and hurtful situations. Although some periods of sadness can be part of stresses in your life, long-term depression can be more serious when the sadness disrupts work, family relations, and affects social, emotional, and physical areas of your life. Regardless of the reason for your depression, if the original emotion is not addressed, the depression will become worse over time. A man was depressed over the loss of the relationship of his first wife many years ago. For years he had a lot of anguish and could not find any joy in life. The sadness was so severe he asked to be let go from his job because he could not function properly at work. It was only when he was able to let go of his hurt, anger, and sadness, that was he able to forgive his ex-wife, himself, and God. To bring a sense of joy back into his life, I asked the man to imagine Jesus hugging him as I prayed for the heavenly Father's love to be poured over him. He began to sob as he was so grateful for the release of his emotional pain and years of depression. He experienced a new joy greater than he had ever felt before. Praise God!

Traditional medical treatment that focuses on the physical or mental symptoms as the primary problem source may have little success when there is suppressed unresolved emotion from the original trauma. The longer the traditional healing attempts are unsuccessful, the faster you will spiral into doubt and discouragement which creates a *crisis of belief.* Over time this crisis will destroy the belief that healing is possible which then creates a shift in thought, attitude, and behavior where the condition consumes your life. Interestingly, you may be a prayer warrior for others, but limit the power of God for your own healing needs. Remember, whether the condition is in the mind or body God has the ability to heal anytime and anywhere He chooses. Your responsibility is to make yourself ready to receive the healing and be obedient to whatever way He chooses to heal. The next section will provide indicators and strategies to break hindrances to healing emotions.

Indicators for Emotional Hindrances

When you follow the healing prayer model and healing still does not happen, it is more common for suppressed emotion to be a potential hindrance. The following are indicators you may want to explore (ask the prayee) to determine if there is unresolved emotion. Conditions of the mind and body that have an emotional origin may be identified by some of the following indicators:

- Injuries that have pain and discomfort that come and go for little or no known reason.

- Aches and pains that appear for no known reason and any pain and discomfort that come and go for little or no known reason.

- Long-term chronic conditions that do not improve with a variety of treatment modalities.

  (Aside from the recommendations in this book, it is suggested to explore other causes to the chronic conditions such as: reactions to medication, food allergies and food additives or environmental issues such as, electric fields, magnetic fields and radio frequencies [EMFs], cell phones, Wi-Fi, mold, etc. For more information regarding environmental and electronic hindrances go to, http://www.createhealthyhomes.com.)

- When there is a feeling of being wronged or an injury by someone or some entity (church, work place, school, or authority figure). This is most evident with indicator statements about feeling unfair, unjust, wronged, angry, hurt, want to get even, or cannot forgive.

- When emotional reactions or the description about the physical condition and cause of condition are talked about as if the incident happened a week ago, when in fact the incident happened a year or more ago.

- When there is a history of experiences or witnessing of others experiencing trauma or abuse. This may include, abuse (such as, physical, mental, emotional, sexual, spiritual, or financial), accidents, military service trauma, loss of an emotionally close relative or pet, witnessing traumatic events, i.e., house burning down, etc.

- When experiencing long-term stressful and/or traumatic situations related to medical, physical, financial, spiritual, occupational, or emotional situations.

If any of the aforementioned indicators are present, you want to ask if they have ever described the incident in detail and expressed emotion from that situation to someone in the past. Most people believe they have "worked through" their trauma, especially if they have gone through forgiveness steps or attended a healing seminar. The truth is when you are hurt at any age, people less often take the time, have the expertise, or have an opportunity to receive undivided attention from someone to compassionately listen to your whole story to release and resolve the emotion at the time of the trauma. As a result, you suppress the feelings and do not realize how the emotion affects your mind, body, and soul. In addition, the more traumatic and the longer you hold in feelings, the more closed you will become about describing the feelings and events as time goes on. Typically, when the prayee has a quick response such as, "Yea, I've dealt with that," or "I've forgiven them," and there is no reference to experiencing an emotional release, the less likely the emotion has been resolved on a deeper level. One important note is that if the traumatic situation or emotion appears to be greater than the prayer minister has knowledge to handle or more than the prayee wants to divulge, I recommend the prayee be referred to a Christian counselor for emotional healing of that situation.

Other causes of suppressed emotion

The following is a list of other potential influences that cause the suppression or lack of emotion. When these influences are in your life, you may have an increased difficulty to receive healing.[11]

- Diet - Certain foods affect your mind causing moodiness, depression, anxiety, etc.

- Depression - Cause symptoms of sadness, suppressed emotion, isolation, and withdrawing socially

- Medication - Side effects may cause moodiness and anxiety

- Sleep deprivation - Impaired judgment, poor concentration and communication skills, slowed reaction times, forgetfulness, and low threshold to express negative emotion

- Attention Deficit Disorder - Difficulty finding feelings, poor attention span, easily distracted, unable to stay focused on a conversation, and poor communicator

- Religious belief (denomination) that discourages the expression of emotions

- Unemotional or emotionally *stuck* personality or way of life

- Living with a spouse (or parents) that are unemotional and/or discourage emotions

---

[11] Craig Miller, *When Your Mate has Emotionally Checked Out* (Mustang, OK: Tate Publishing, 2006).

> ## PART TWO
> ### FINDING VICTORY IN HEALING PRAYER

Chapter 4

Strategies with Children and Persevering through Prayer

CRAIG MILLER

When you pray for a child and healing doesn't happen, it can be one of the most disappointing, frustrating, and helpless experiences. God does not want you to be a victim to a belief of powerlessness and hopelessness, but rather He wants you to become victorious in His power by persevering in His presence and authority. The following is an effective strategy to persevere in your ministering with others.

Changing caregiver attitudes and atmospheres

Caring for a sick child brings a multitude of emotional responses that are often suppressed or denied by caregivers as a way to cope with the difficult situation and shield the child from their emotions. Without being aware, these suppressed feelings can come out through attitudes, frustrations, short tempers, unhealthy words, and non-verbal expressions that are received by the child. In turn, the child will internalize these reactions and convert them into self-destructive beliefs such as, "I'm a burden," "This condition is my fault," "I'm doing something wrong," etc. If the child takes on these beliefs or the burden of the condition, healing prayer can be hindered. The caregiver should be strongly encouraged to have an emotional support system (including daily prayer time) in order to frequently verbalize their feelings and concerns without affecting the child. This may include regular meetings with a mentor, friend, healing team, pastoral staff, or a professional counselor.

A young boy had physical and emotional disabilities that were not progressing in rehabilitation therapy. When I spoke with the mother, I could see the despair and disappointment on her face from lack of progress over the years. Although the mother reassured me she was careful not to show her emotions around the child, her frustration came through with her responses. When I helped the mother identify and release her feelings of anger, and when she stopped blaming herself, she was able to relax about her son's situation and show more compassion. As a result, her son stopped feeling blamed for his illness and was able to progress in his healing through prayer and treatment.

Children are typically mirrors of what is happening around them and respond to the atmosphere from what the caregivers and authority figures create. If the caregivers are anxious, doubting, negative, or struggle to believe in healing, then the child will often have the same tendencies. If healing doesn't happen with the child, privately ask the parents about their expectation for healing and determine if they have hindrances that are influencing the child's healing. I suggest you meet with the caregivers to work through any personal hindrances or issues that may be influencing the child.

There was a boy in his late teens who had a terminal condition and had received prayer over the years with minimal change. When the condition became worse I called the father about praying for his son and asked to bring others that had been healed of the same condition. After a brief silence the father said, "This condition is not the same, it can't be cured. I don't want it to be more discouraging...if God doesn't heal him." I was surprised by the father's unwillingness to give God another opportunity to bring healing. In my discouragement I simply said I would keep him in my prayers and offered to pray with his son if he changed his mind. Caregivers can have the greatest influence to determine a child's healing destiny.

In his teaching, *The Agony of Defeat,* Dr. Randy Clark emphasizes that we need to be humble and loving in our approach to healing, especially when healing doesn't happen. Humility and the willingness to say "I don't know" prevent us from letting our "failure" experiences define our beliefs, heading us into the downward spiral of unbelief. In addition, we should always minister in love. If we minister in love, even if no healing manifests, we will have brought His life to those in need. It is more important to "love God and be known by God" than to have the answers when failure in healing comes our way.[12]

Conditions from past generations

It is important that you pray to break the condition, or curse and spirit from the condition, that may be transferred to the child from the mother, the father, and generations before them. A mother told me her family doctor was very concerned when he heard a heart murmur in her four year old child. The mother asked for healing prayer before she took the boy to his appointment with a heart specialist for an evaluation and treatment. Since we were aware of a possible generational heart condition, we asked

---

[12] For more information see: Clark, *School of Healing and Impartation Workbook.*

God to break off any generational heart conditions and we prayed for a new, healthy heart from heaven. When the boy became extremely hot all over his body, we knew God was performing His healing. A week later we were told the heart specialist examined the boy's heart and found nothing wrong. Praise God! For strategies to release curses with the child or caregivers, use the information found in the section named Curses under Section III.

Utero, birth, and early childhood trauma

When healing is hindered it is important to consider what happened medically, mentally, and emotionally to the child during the stages of utero, birth, and early childhood. Starting at approximately the sixth month, the unborn child can see, feel, taste, hear, and sense whether they are safe, loved, or wanted. For example, studies have shown that women trapped in a stormy marriage run a 237 percent greater risk of bearing a psychologically or physically damaged child compared to a woman in a secure, nurturing relationship.[13] Studies also show trauma associated with the birthing process such as forced delivery or prolonged time in the birth canal may create more life anxieties;[14] and an unstable, neglectful, or chaotic early childhood environment may create fears and insecurities that may impede healing prayer. If you detect or suspect early trauma to the child, pray the following:

In the authority of Jesus Christ I break off the emotional or physical trauma of (name trauma if known) *to the body, mind, and spirit.*

Next, pray the following prayer to replace what was sent away.

---

[13] For more information see: Dr. Thomas Verny, *The Secret Life of the Unborn Child* (New York, NY: Dell Publishing, 1982).

[14] For more information see: Dr. Thomas Verny, *Tomorrow's Baby* (New York, NY: Simon & Schuster, 2002).

In the name of Jesus Christ I ask the heavenly Father for a healthy _____. Thank you for Your peace, love, and the blood of Jesus Christ as a covering for total healing and wholeness of mind, body, and spirit.

Demonic influence

It is important to consider evil influences or spirits as a potential cause if healing does not happen. These influences usually come from the atmosphere they live in and/or the caregivers. This can include evil influences that are transferred from your lifestyle, spirits that are transferred by generational curses and beliefs, or influences from the atmosphere (see Chapter 8, Changing the Atmosphere to Believe in Your Healing). You can utilize many of the same strategies found with the information about Spiritual Warfare in Section III. If you do not feel comfortable when praying for someone with potential spiritual warfare issues, refer the person to someone with more experience. A four year old boy was diagnosed with epileptic seizures and had little change in his condition with medical treatment and prayer. When the parents took the boy for deliverance, the demonic presence was cast out and the condition was totally healed. Praise God!

Persevering Through the Power in the Cross

In his teaching, *The Agony of Defeat,* Dr. Randy Clark emphasizes that in healing we are entering into a warfare dimension of the cross and must prepare ourselves in the power of God. As a result, we need to be empowered by God to be able to keep persevering in the ministry of healing.[15] During your most difficult times when healing doesn't happen is when you need to become the closest to God and seek ways to persevere

---

[15] For more information see: Clark, *School of Healing and Impartation Workbook.*

beyond your personal point of experience and knowledge to allow God to bring more victories. Below are prayer interventions to assist in your perseverance. For additional information seek guidance through pastoral counsel or a healing prayer team.

- **Seeking the anointing of the Holy Spirit** (1 John 2:27, 2 Corinthians 4:7) Pray for God to anoint you with the Holy Spirit. The anointing is God's Spirit and power for service on this earth. Jesus has provided the same presence of the Holy Spirit for us in our earthly ministries that He had in His earthly ministry.

- **Fasting and prayer** (Mark 9:29) Spend a period of time giving up or sacrificing something and spend that time praying with God about the healing needs.

- **Intercessory prayer** (James 5:16) Ask the elders of a church and/or other Christians (that believe in the healing power of prayer) to pray for healing.

- **Anointing with oil** (James 5:14) Anointing oil represents the Holy Spirit. Touch the prayee with oil as you pray for healing. You can purchase anointing oil or use any oil that is sanctified (prayed over in the name of Jesus Christ as anointing oil).

- **Prayer cloths** (Acts 19:11-12) Anoint a small cloth or handkerchief with your words of healing and give the cloth to the prayee to put on their body.

Chapter 5
Inner Healing
DR. RANDY CLARK

I have been in ministry for over forty-three years, a pastor for over thirty. In my years of pastoring, I have heard and seen so much, including pain. I have seen some people that it seems like no matter what I tell them, they never change. I wonder well, why is that? I think we can get some of those answers in light of the understanding that comes from the ministry of "inner healing," which is also known as the "healing of emotions," and is in my belief part of the process of sanctification.

In my life, my father was also a good man, a hard worker. He worked in the oil fields and farmed on the side, and worked eighty hours a week most of his life before he retired. He worked hard to provide for us food and shelter, and the way that he showed his love was by providing. I cannot remember him really showing emotion though until he got older. When I was a child growing up I played sports. My dad wanted to attend these events, but as I mentioned he worked so much, he would hardly have time. He would say, "I want to be there," and I remember in high school particularly, in the Freshman and Sophomore year, playing basketball, looking up into the bleachers to see if dad made it. I never questioned his love, his provision, his acceptance of me, of his being pleased with me. I never questioned those things, but where I dealt with the issue was: can I depend on him showing up? I had a personal issue that I struggled with. I was very insecure. It was difficult for me to believe that if I said, "Come, Holy Spirit," He would. If John Wimber did, He would. If Benny Hinn did, He would. If Kathryn Kuhlman did, He would, and so on with a number of others. However, if Randy Clark said, "Come, Holy Spirit," He might.

Even when I was getting ready to go to Toronto (prior to what would become known as the "Toronto Blessing") people would say, "What do you think is going to happen when you go to Toronto?" Even after we had these major outpourings of the Spirit, the regional meetings at the Vineyard at my Church from August to January, we had been having visitations every week just like what was happening in Toronto. Actually, Toronto was just when it caught the people's eye, but it happened in a Regional Meeting, it had been happening in my home church since that August. People would say, "Well, what do you think is going to happen when you go to Toronto?" I would say, "Well, I hope God shows up," and even my own oldest son who was twelve years old at the time said, "Dad, you don't have any faith." I knew my problem was that I doubted. I still believed I could say, "Come, Holy Spirit," and He might, just might, show up.

I began to be used in Toronto, and I spent much time with John and Carol Arnott. One day while in Toronto, I was driving down the road with Carol Arnott and another guy. Carol had seen how insecure I was.

She had seen me "fish" for compliments. I think too, the Lord just told her I needed to be rid of my insecurity.

While we were driving, I will never forget it, she said, "You did well in school, didn't you?"

I said, "Yes, I did. You know, Honor Rolls, Dean's list."

She said, "Did you feel driven to do well?"

I said, "Yeah, I wanted to do well."

She said, "Why do you think you were that way? And do you care what people think about you?"

I said, "Oh, yes, too much. That is a hook of mine; I really want to be accepted. I have a need for attention. I have a need to hear somebody to say you did well, and I have a need to do well. When I was in school, I had a great need to make A's."

She said, "Why do you think you are that way?"

I said, "Well, I have got it figured out. You see my dad only had an eighth grade education, my grandmother was illiterate, and I was the first boy to go past the eighth grade in our family line. My dad wanted us to do well in school, so he offered us a dollar. Now, a dollar back in grade school, around 1958, was a lot more than it is today. I got a dollar for every A. B's did not count, and anything lower than a B, I would have got to give back a dollar. So that's why I needed to do well," I said.

I then went on to tell Carol, "I got $10 for being on the Honor Roll. So, that's why I am that way; I have got it figured out."

She replied, "Well I don't think that has anything to do with it."

When she said that, it blew me away because I thought that the reason why I was this way about performance orientation was because of this programming as a boy, and I really thought that was it.

She went on, "Why do you think that has anything to do with it? Do you fish for compliments?"

I said, "I hate to admit it, but yes, and I'm pretty good at it, too."

She said, "Do you really get upset about justice issues?"

I said, "Yes; I get very upset at injustice."

Then she said, "Are you so extremely modest that it is kind of—you know, weird?"

I said, "Yeah, I guess I am."

She said again, "Well why do you think you're that way?"

I thought, then said, "Well now I don't know."

So Carol went on, "You were conceived out of wedlock, weren't you?"

Taken aback, I replied, "Yes, but that was my mom and dad's sin, that doesn't have anything to do with me. They asked for forgiveness, and then they got married."

Then Carol told me, "That has everything to do with your issues."

At times, I felt I was broken in spirit, but what does that mean? Could it be something like the Beattitudes? Blessed are those who are poor in spirit? Could it be that those who recognize their brokenness, their insufficiency. The place of vulnerability and need is very important for those who recognize that they desperately need the touch of God. David's understanding of the sacrifices of God is in his honesty and his coming to a place of just realizing that he is broken and needs God to put him back together. He truly has a broken and contrite heart. This passage gave me an understanding of mercy. I thought, "God, I get it! I get it!" I now understand why and how You can be so merciful, because when I did not understand or why I was thinking and acting the way I was, You still did. You knew me better than I knew me.

Through inner healing, I realized that I was not born with a clean slate. I found out my will was not nearly as free as I had thought. In Hebrew, the meaning of sin is this: you are walking along a slippery path, and you are trying your hardest not to fall, but you slip and fall. That word is one of the meanings of sin. It does not have to be intentional. That is why the holiness understanding of sin is a violation of God's will. Actually, it deals with transgression, and it is quoting from the New Testament, but the Old Testament understanding goes deeper than that. Sin is not necessarily something that you planned or willed to do. You could have been trying your hardest but slipped and fell. That is often called in holiness circles "weakness" or "mistakes." Then the word iniquity means that from birth, you were born with a nature that is twisted that you inherited from your parents. It is as if it were hereditary; this is the word iniquity, there is something flawed in character from birth.

God has an infinite understanding of every human being, and when we do not understand that strong drive, even toward sin, our wills are not near as free as what we think. Inner healing is a way of going through the process of sanctification and becoming what God says we are. We are free, forgiven, and He wants to make us even freer. Inner healing can happen in different ways. It can happen just as you go about life—you get the right word at the right time. That word fitly spoken, that right time, the right word at the right time can set people free, and that is what we want, to all become better at doing that.

Sometimes inner healing happens in a counseling session. Sometimes inner healing can happen just by God sovereignly revealing something to you, and sometimes inner healing can happen through prophecy. A lot of prophetic ministry has an inner healing aspect to it. Just like how words of knowledge deals with healing of the physical body, prophetic ministry often is bringing healing to the soul and dealing with how you perceive yourself. It also involves how you perceive others, and even how you perceive God. A revelation can often come to a prophetic word, and that is why I think Paul had such a value on prophecy because he saw the power of prophecy to express the love of God, to build up, to comfort, and to encourage.

God wants us to experience the freedom that He gives us, and that is what the whole process of the Church is meant to be in sanctification. So, this was one of the things that was okay for me—because of God's understanding, He knows. Because He knows, that is why He is so merciful. Now, when it comes to our relationship with God, we understand that justice is getting what you deserve, mercy is not getting what you deserve, and grace is getting more than you deserve (in a positive sense). However, grace is more than undeserved forgiveness. Grace is more than even getting gifts that we do not deserve. One of the main meanings of grace in the New Testament is a divine enablement. We need this grace of God at work in our lives and with the people that we count on. We need to believe that God is willing to give us divine enablement beyond our human capacity.

Grace that comes beyond us from God is not only to forgive the sin, but it is also to give us the power to live differently. With grace there needs to come truth. Until we get some understandings of truths, it is harder for this grace to bring about the full work that God wants in our life because we are actually believing the lie of the enemy rather than the truth of God. This is where theology is important.

My wife and I experienced freedom in a lot of different ways, through ministry that is called inner healing, a ministry that sometimes has been misunderstood. Sometimes people do not even think you need inner healing. They may think it is not even really biblical, but I think it is. I think it deals with the whole issue of maturing, becoming more like Jesus, getting free—it is all utter sanctification. What else is sanctification about if it is not becoming freer to be who God wants you to be? It is more than an experience. It is a life of experiences that are changing as you are applying the truth of God's word and making yourself available to the grace of the Spirit.

I know personally the value of inner healing ministry and the importance of it. It is my desire that all believers will become people that are liberators of other people—in your family, in yourself, and in your Church. I am no longer so driven, not the way I used to be. I am not totally healed yet, but I am freer than I ever was, and I thank God for the freedom. I do have a lot of plates and spin a lot of things while I travel the world, but God knows my heart. Some my highest goals include being a good father, husband, and a good man because if you have all of these other accomplishments but you have failed as a father, failed as a husband, and failed at just being a good person of integrity, the other stuff does not really mean anything.

I think to say that we do not need inner healing, or if you are a Christian that you cannot be bothered by the demonic, it sounds like that would be a good word, except if in reality you are fighting these battles and losing them. You repent and lose, and repent and lose, and you wonder why you cannot get victory. If you believe that the reason is because you do not understand the truth or have enough willpower, then you can get pretty hopeless, but if you understand that your sin may be bigger than you, then it becomes more manageable. You cannot control your will if you realize that is not completely free. It is comforting when you struggle to know that your will can be quite in bondage sometimes, and it is good news to know that there can be a way of getting free!

I want to pray for your freedom now,

Father, sometimes we have said, 'Lord, make me like an instrument, play me any way You want in the sense of giving Words of Knowledge and Prophecies and things,' but Lord, we also want to say, 'Lord, to make our lives an open book and point to anything you want, and show us areas where You want to heal us this week.' Give us greater understanding, and if we don't have any issues, then help us to have a better understanding of other peoples' issues. O Lord, let us have Your ear to hear as Moses heard the Lord say to him, I have seen the affliction of My people and I have come down, and I am sending you. May we believe that You still hear the cries of the people when they are all by themselves and they are desperate, and they cry out and they wonder, Why can't I change? Lord, may we believe that You do hear those cries and You have come down to say to us, and I am sending you. Give us mercy and grace toward ourselves. Give us that broken spirit that cries out: 'I need You, Your Divine Empowerment.' Break off of us deceptions. Bring in to light, things that have been hidden in darkness, or at least hidden from our own understanding, and show us the steps we can take to cooperate with Your Grace, that the spiritual principles under which this world operates just as it does natural principles would take effect in our lives and we would be free. In the Name of Jesus. Amen.

Chapter 6
Strategies for Emotional Healing
CRAIG MILLER

In his book, *Mind Body Prescription,* Dr. John Sarno, MD comments that when emotions become overwhelming the mind produces physical symptoms to keep your attention focused on the body to avoid the feelings that are so unbearable.[16] The longer the emotions are suppressed and continue to be unresolved, the longer the physical condition will remain to divert attention away from the original emotional source. In essence, when your emotions are suppressed, there is a disconnect between your body, mind, and spirit. This is among the reasons inner healing is so important for the healing of the body and mind.

---

[16] For more information see: John Sarno, *Mind Body Prescription* (New York, NY: Time Warner, 1998), 18.

A woman in her late sixties told me about her years of depression and a variety of medical problems that were not getting better with more treatment. When I asked God to reveal what the issue was in her life that brought the most emotional pain, what came to mind was the death of her special needs child many years ago. The Lord led me to instruct the woman to forgive herself for "failing as a mother," and to ask for forgiveness for being angry at God. I instructed the woman to think about Jesus hugging her and Jesus telling her the following, "I love you and you are forgiven. I will take care of your son and you don't need to worry about him anymore." The woman cried as she released the pain and received God's love. When the woman opened her eyes she had the biggest smile on her face. She felt released from depression and free to begin healing from her medical conditions. Praise God!

In another case, a woman described having overwhelming anxiety for years when something negative would happen or there was conflict with someone. Over the last six years she had daily panic attacks. The medication she took would only temporarily soothe the anxiety and worry. During prayer, God took her back to six years old when a brother who was babysitting pointed their father's gun to her head. As she released the emotion from that original trauma and she envisioned Jesus bringing His love and protection to the little girl, the anxiety vanished. When the woman once more described the incident, it was only a memory without any anxiety. She was also unable to feel any anxiety that she would typically experience as an adult. Praise God!

What these people, and countless others have in common is the lack of opportunity to identify and release the emotion from the original event. In addition, when your feelings are not allowed or heard, your emotions become suppressed and you do not feel encouraged or safe to express yourself. It is your primary caregiver's responsibility to give unconditional love and create a safe environment for your protection and ability to express emotion. As a result, when you are hurt by others and your feelings are not allowed you feel insignificant and unloved. This creates the belief that if your feelings are not good enough then you must not be good enough to receive the good things God has for your life, such as healing. Consequently, if you believe your parents do not think you are important, then God must not think you are important. This distorted belief can be produced any time in life but becomes the strongest during childhood hurts and neglect when your belief about yourself is the most vulnerable.

Inner healing is more than just forgiveness. It is allowing your soul (mind, body, and emotions) to continually become free from the worldly negative influences (Romans 12:1-2) and allowing to release the negative emotion that should not be owned to you (Ephesians 4: 22-24, 26, 31). Inner healing is creating the healthy belief that you are loved by God, that you are good enough to be loved, and that your feelings are good enough to be expressed and heard. This ultimately fosters the belief that if you are good enough for God you are good enough to receive the healing God has for you.

God created you with feelings as a natural way to communicate with others your innermost desires, needs, and reactions to what is happening. Living any other way is not living to the fullest of what God originally created. Dr. Bernie S. Siegel, MD, explained it the best about the importance of expressing emotions when he wrote in his book, *Peace, Love and Healing*, "It's important to express all your feelings, including the unpleasant ones, because once they're out they lose their power over you; they can't tie you up in knots anymore. Letting them out is a call for help and a 'live' message to your body."[17] Emotional expression opens the pathway to releasing internal energy to free the mind and body to heal. Whereas suppressed emotion blocks the pathway to emotional energy release diverting the internal energy to release through physical symptoms.

---

[17] For more information see: Bernie S. Siegel, *Peace, Love and Healing* (New York, NY: HarperCollins, 1989).

Once the emotions are identified and released, the body is no longer in bondage to that emotion and release of the physical symptoms can begin. It may be the case that your prayers are ineffective because the emotional or traumatic memory holds the body or mind hostage to the physical or mental condition. After a period of time with unsuccessful treatment, you have two choices: You can either become discouraged that nothing will ever happen, or you can become extremely motivated to seek out more of God to make something happen.

A forty-six year old woman had liver pain for two months. She woke up at night with severe pain and sweats and nausea every night. She experienced no energy, poor sleep, not feeling well, forcing herself to do things, and generally it was difficult to get through the day. She was told by doctors her liver enzymes were up which caused most of the sickness. At first she was reluctant about praying for her healing. However, she later admitted to being tired of living this way which was her motivation to allow me to pray with her. The next night after we prayed for God's healing, she slept better, there was no pain, her energy was up, and she had more motivation. She later said, "I have better moods. The more I do, the better I feel and the more I'm not the same!" Praise God!

You must always believe that God, your Great Physician, has the ability to heal anything, anytime, anywhere. However, the original unhealthy emotion is not released, the condition may return, creating the belief that prayers do not work. There was a woman who received neck and upper back injuries from an auto accident a year earlier. When we prayed for healing the pain disappeared believing she was healed. A week later she reported the pain had returned even though she prayed against the pain. This time I asked God to take her back to envision the original injury. As the woman described the incident in more detail, before, during, and after the accident, she released thet emotional trauma from those memories. When she was done releasing the emotion, the pain was permanently gone and all we needed to do was thank Jesus for the healing that took place without asking for it. Praise God!

There are many forms of inner healing that are available. To try and make it more understandable, inner healing primarily covers areas such as: the emotion from the original hurt, distorted beliefs created from those hurts, sins and curses of the past, unforgiveness, and any demonic issues or oppression. As Randy mentioned there are many ways to receive inner healing and there are also many Christian ministries that provide some form of inner healing. However, in regards to emotional and physical healing, since eight-five percent of body ailments have an emotional element, identifying and releasing emotion is very important because the suppression of emotion is more common than people realize. Simply telling your story of past events and identifying what your condition makes you feel can have a major impact on your ability to be healed. The following strategies can help to identify and release emotion that may be hindering your healing.

If you have a physical or emotional condition and do not know the cause, review Suggested Emotional Connection to Body/Mind Conditions found in Chapter Nine. Follow the instructions listed with the chart and then use the following technique Heart Transformation for Emotional Healing found below.

If you are aware of a past traumatic event or know the cause of a condition and want to release emotion from those issues, you can also follow the Heart Transformation for Emotional Healing technique below.

Heart Transformation for Emotional Healing

I. RECOGNIZE the emotion—TWO OPTIONS
[Prayee closes eyes throughout steps]

Option A. If the cause of the condition is identified, ask or tell the prayee . . .

Describe what happened and identify your feelings as a result of that situation (Describe as many feelings as possible, i.e., sad, discouraged, failure . . .)

Are you ready to let go of your feelings? If yes, prayee places hands on heart (If no, talk about the situation/feelings until they feel emotion or are ready to let go).

Picture Jesus with you. (go to RELEASE)

Option B. If there is no clear cause for the condition, ask the prayee . . .

Describe the feelings as a result of living with this condition.
(Describe as many feelings as possible i.e., sad, discouraged, stuck, useless . . .)

Where do you feel this emotion in your body? i.e., stomach, heart, head, legs, arms . . .

When the prayee identifies where the emotion is felt in the body, pray the following…

Holy Spirit take (prayee name) in their past to where they first felt this way in their life.

When the prayee reveals earlier memory/emotion, ask or tell the prayee . . .

Describe what happened and identify your feelings during that time in your life.

Do you feel those feelings now and where do you feel them? (If no, talk about situation until they feel emotions.)

Are you ready to let go of the feelings? If yes, prayee places hands on their heart. (If no, talk about the situation/feelings until they feel emotion or are ready to let go).

Picture Jesus with you. (go to RELEASE)

II. RELEASE [Ask prayee to repeat the following]

In Jesus name . . .

I see this emotion as a spirit; I will not allow this spirit to be a part of me anymore.

I release this spirit to Jesus and command it go
(Imagine giving the spirit to Jesus).

And in its place I receive from my heavenly Father, His Spirit of _____ (i.e., love, peace, truth, healing, etc.), *And I put these into my heart. Thank you Jesus for my healing.*

[Optional] *Jesus, is there anything you want (prayee's name) to see or hear about this situation?*

III. REPENT and forgive [Ask prayee to repeat the following]

I repent for allowing (name emotion) to be a part of my life.

I forgive (<u>offender's name</u>) for what they said/did to me.

In Jesus name I will not allow (<u>offender's name</u>) to control me through this feeling.
[Optional] *God, forgive me for believing You* _____
(<u>...didn't protect me, let it happen..., etc.</u>)

What are you feeling and seeing now?
(If the emotion/condition is still present repeat steps I thru III)

IV. REFILL the heart [Ask or tell the prayee the following]

As you see yourself with Jesus in your mind, can Jesus give you a hug?

Picture Jesus giving you a hug (Ask prayee to cross arms across chest or hold a pillow)

Pray the following with the prayee:

Father in heaven, thank you for giving (prayee's name) your love. Fill them with Your love from the top of their head to the bottom of their feet. Fill (prayee's name) with (give positive feelings).
In Jesus name.

Ask, *What do you feel or see now?* (Continue steps for each condition or past event or if emotions from condition or past events continue to be present.)

If feelings cannot be identified or resolved, seek assistance with a Christian counselor experienced in uncovering past hurts, releasing suppressed emotion, and revealing God's truth.

For a printable copy of Heart Transformation for Emotional Healing, go to the Healing Information page on the website, www.feelingsbook.com

Chapter 7

Why You Lose Your Healing and How to Keep It

CRAIG MILLER

Witnessing God's power when someone becomes healed is an exciting experience while in comparison to hearing about someone losing their healing can be very disappointing. Since everyone is at a different understanding and acceptance with how God's power works, you will need to be prepared to see a variety of responses to your prayers, especially when someone loses their healing. Speaker and author Andrew Wommack has quoted the great crusade healer, Kathryn Kuhlman as saying that only ten to fifteen percent of people keep their healing. This is a very revealing and discouraging statistic because in reality it can be far too easy to lose your healing than it should be. The good news is, as a loving heavenly Father,

God loves you too much to take away something He has given to glorify His name. Consequently, you must be honest with the condition of our heart, mind, and body to determine the reason for losing your healing. This chapter will highlight reasons why you can lose your healing and ways to become secure in your healing experience.

Some reasons you lose your healing

When you physically experience a return of the original condition your mind may begin to doubt your healing and question your belief about the prayer you received. What you believe and how you react to your healing is the pivotal point of what happens next—whether you lose or keep your healing. What you do with your thoughts and symptoms has to do with your own understanding of: faith, expectations, God's Word, spiritual/emotional support, lifestyle, and unresolved emotion.

Level of faith

Out of uncertainty, without knowing it, your mind can become consumed by the return of a symptom. The more you think about the returning symptom, the more you may let go of the healing as your mind becomes consumed with what may happen. This is especially true if you have become accustomed to living with a condition for many years and/or your level of faith is not strong enough to believe in something greater than what you understand or are accustomed to living. It would be normal to establish a lifestyle to compensate for a specific condition or life of pain. Changing a lifestyle in an instant can be hard to do when you are instantly healed. It only takes twenty-eight days of doing the same thing for it to become a habit. The habit then becomes your patterning of living life. Then the patterning becomes your identity. As odd as it may seem, you can be so accustomed to living with a condition that the freedom from your pain can be unusual and even make you more fearful.

You may say how much you desire to be free but your fear of failing or changing from years of what you have known can ironically be stronger than your desire. You develop emotional and physical patterns of how to live with a condition and become dependent on those patterns as a way to cope with the stresses of life. This type of healing starts through the inner healing of those issues that keep you afraid to change rather than focusing on your physical condition.

This is also true for your level of faith. Since faith is based on hoping something will happen beyond your understanding (Hebrews 11:1), it can be difficult to step into a new level of belief that God has healed you while you are still experiencing pain. Even though God's love and healing power is greater than the returning symptom, you revert back to your understanding or comfort level of faith based on what you believe is to be true from your life experiences. This tends to be the case if you have not achieved a level of faith that can believe in something that does not feel, look, smell, or sound like it is healed. It can be difficult to step up to a new level of belief that something will happen if that experience is beyond your level of understanding.

The pastor at a church where my wife and I were ministering asked us to make a special trip to the home of an elderly woman for healing prayer. At the home the woman had severe neck and shoulder pain from a fall many months earlier. Over the months she had various medical treatments, but confessed they did little to stop the pain. We prayed with her for over an hour. Each time we prayed we asked how much better she felt on a scale from zero to hundred percent. She slowly improved each time at twenty, fifty, then eighty-five percent better. Each time she showed much caution and verbalized some doubt as we ministered. Before we left, I explained the need to continue exercising her faith, asking her to keep thanking Jesus for her healing. One week later we called her to see how she was doing. Her first words were, "It didn't do any good, the pain is back. I wasn't healed." My first instinct was to protest by exclaiming,

Yes, you were healed! But I didn't. I calmly asked what happened. She was not accustomed to God working through healing prayer and did not have enough understanding to know what to do to combat the return of the pain. Normally, I would continue to pray with the person to bind the returned pain but I felt God wanted me to give a simple prayer and encourage her not to give up praying.

In situations such as this it is important to respect the person's level of understanding and desire about praying. Wait for God to lead you to either *push in* for more healing prayer or encourage the person with a simple *prayer of encouragement* by telling them to keep praying and that God loves them. It is easy to be discouraged with these situations, as my wife and I were with this woman. However, we realized it is our job to plant the seed and allow the Holy Spirit to do the rest. So I recommend you reassure others that God is still in the business of healing and He will honor your prayer requests in His time and in His way.

Level of expectation

Keeping your healing can also be greatly influenced by your level of need and expectation for heavenly intervention. In affluent countries where there are many resources, healing is only a credit card away, and God is often sought only as the last resort. When I was ministering in less affluent countries we were all amazed how receptive people were to our prayers and how quickly people were healed with simple requests to God. After one church service a family approached me and the mother simply pointed to the eyes of her six year old daughter. I called an interpreter over to me and found out the girl was wearing glasses because she could not see words close up without them being blurry. I asked the girl to take off her glasses as I prayed over the eyes and claimed healing in the name of Jesus. When I asked her to read something she was able to see better. Praise God! The girl simply believed what Jesus could do. The team members and I talked about why it seemed so different in the United States where people did not show the same receptivity and why the same quick results did not often manifest. We concluded that when there is a greater dependence on something beyond your means there creates a greater belief in what God can do and a greater expectation that His power will meet those needs.

When people put prayer at the bottom of a list of healing options there is less expectation for God to heal. Although I am very much in favor of God using health professionals for healing purposes, I believe God just wants to be number one in consideration. I have prayed with many people who have either scheduled or plan to schedule medical intervention for their condition and amazingly seen God miraculously heal them hours before medical treatment. And at the same time, I have also experienced people become healed, then lose their healing and quickly choose a medical intervention without considering the fact they were healed and do not try to regain the healing.

Two years prior to meeting Jane, she was diagnosed with arthritis in her hip. Over that period of time she had severe pain and finally decided to have surgery that was scheduled in the next three weeks. Since I was aware that the emotional root cause of arthritis can originate from resentment and bitterness, we spent time releasing the unresolved emotion and unforgiveness from past abuse. When I asked God for healing, the arthritis pain was gone and the shorter leg became even with the other. She jogged around the house with no pain, no tenderness, and no limp. Jane was overjoyed! Praise God! When I made a follow up call a week later she told me the pain was back. She said she was tired of living with the pain and decided to continue with the surgery. At this point, there was not much room for changing her mind, so I encouraged her with prayer and asked God's blessing over her.

Jane had made up her mind and wanted nothing to do with praying again. She had an alternate plan she wanted to pursue. I tried not to show my disappointment as I gave her a *prayer of encouragement* regarding the situation. If the person you are praying for is willing to receive prayer up to the time of medical intervention, continue to pray and believe in God's healing power up to and during the treatment process if necessary. As I have continued to pray with people through the process of medical interventions, I have witnessed God use various professionals as His instruments for healing. The fact that the prayee does not receive healing during your initial prayer should not be seen as the end but rather an opportunity to see what God wants to do in His timing and with whomever or whatever circumstances He puts in the person's path.

Understanding of God's Word

It is often the case that people will have a hard time believing what the Bible says is the same for them today. When Jesus said, ". . . all things for which you pray and ask, believe that you have received them, and they will be *granted* you" Mark 11:24, He wants you to believe exactly what He said. This is done by thinking and acting in the belief you have been healed through everything you do. It can be helpful to read healing scriptures as often as you can for the renewing of your mind and to believe in your heart the truth for your life.

Also, it is also important to remember anything you receive from God will be contested by the devil because the devil doesn't want you to have it! Receiving healing or a miracle is no different. "Resist the devil and he will flee from you," (James 4:7). How do you resist him? With your faith in the Word of God stating that what you received is yours to keep. For example, think that you are really battling more than just a sickness, but a force of evil that does not want you healed. So when you pray to send away the pain, remember you have already been given God's gift of healing and you can tell the enemy, the evil force, to leave and take the pain with him. Just speak in the authority given to you, saying, *In Jesus name I send this pain away.*

Lack of spiritual/emotional support

When you are emotionally or physically hurting, some of the best medicine is words of wisdom, comforting touches, and prayers for healing. It is natural for you to seek the wisdom and comfort of someone that can satisfy your needs when you are hurting. However, when you do not have emotional and spiritual support from people in your life, you will find it more difficult to remain encouraged and sustain your healing. A 1995 study at Dartmouth-Hitchcock Medical Center found that one of the best predictors of survival among 232 heart-surgery patients was the degree to which the patients said they drew comfort and strength from religious faith. Those who did not draw comfort and strength from religious faith had more than three times the death rate of those who did.

One key to sustaining your healing is where and how you keep your focus. If you waiver away from God's promises and use former patterns of thinking and behaving, it may be a struggle to keep what you gained. This is especially true if you have lived with a condition for years and you are not accustomed to the positive change. Without the encouragement of caring support you can easily waver into former habits that pull you back to negative thinking and behaviors.

There was a woman that lived alone and was unable to travel outside her home because of her debilitating neurological condition. When my wife and I prayed every other week for God to bring healing for the pain, swelling, shaking, and numbness in her arms and legs, she would feel and walk better each time we finished prayer. When we met with her the next time she would be emotionally discouraged and had reverted back to the physical condition that we prayed during our prior visit. At first we were baffled as to why she was not keeping her healing from one visit to the next. After several visits we came to realize she had no support in between our visits to encourage her. She could only rely on her own thoughts and ability and could not sustain what she gained the week before. In situations of poor support it is important to explore ways to connect people with resources such as phone calls, visits, prayer lines, greeting cards, emails, and any other ways to keep the person encouraged.

Lifestyle

It is often the case that when issues in life such as general health habits and lifestyle are not changed, there is a greater likelihood that you can lose the healing. For example, when a woman was healed of diabetes, she felt good physically and began to eat all the foods she could not eat when she had the condition of diabetes. Unfortunately, six months later her diabetes condition returned. One assumption we can make is that her unhealthy food choices had a major influence in her condition returning.

In another example, I suffered intermittently from lower back pain for thirty years. There was one particular weekend when the pain was extremely bad and my prayers did not seem to make a difference. Since my wife and I just happened to be attending a new church that had an invitation for healing, I hobbled forward to become miraculously healed. Even when I continue to praise God for my healing, I have realized that some pain would occasionally return when I did not perform daily exercises. Among the reasons I was able to survive all those years when I did have back problems was through stretching and walking every morning. After God healed my back, I realized stretching and walking each morning was still the best way to maintain what I had gained through my healing and a way to continue feeling better physically and sleeping better at night.

Although you may want to encourage the prayee to be wise about how they live out their healing, it is important not to give medical or health advice. For example, if a person was healed of a medical condition or chronic pain, you should never tell the person to stop taking their medication or change their medical requirements until they consult with the health professional responsible for their medical care.

Unresolved emotion

As I mentioned in a previous chapter, when trauma happens in your life there is a succession of changes to our mind, body, and spirit. Over time, the suppressed emotions in your body and mind can begin to manifest as physical and mental symptoms. It is often the case that healing prayer will eliminate the immediate symptoms. However, emotion stored in flesh, cells, muscles, tendons, posture, organs, and memories will return because the original emotion held inside was not released. A woman slipped and fell on a wet floor while she was at work. She injured her hip and received a slight head concussion from the fall. Over twenty years later she was still experiencing severe pain in her back and down her legs. When I prayed for God to bring healing, the pain immediately left and she walked away pain free. Praise God! When I saw her a week later most of the pain had returned. She was very discouraged and had a lot of doubt about her healing as she was told by her doctor she had to live with the condition the rest of her life. I had her imagine and recount the experiences from the moment of the accident to weeks after the accident. As she described the events I continuously had her describe her feelings. As the feelings were released, her pain eventually disappeared without having to pray for her.

To understand why the woman's pain returned you must realize she had layers of suppressed emotions that still needed to be released. She had the emotional pain of embarrassment, loss of her job, loss of wages, lack of support from the company, anger, bitterness, misunderstanding of family, unforgiveness, and the list goes on. Once those suppressed emotions and unforgiveness issues were released the pain was able to be released. Praise God!

Because of His love, God wants to give what you ask for. Although this is great news for anyone wanting healing, God also gave you freedom of choice to decide what to do with depression, resentment, bitterness, pride, unforgiveness, and countless other issues that can influence the desire of your healing. The choice is yours to make.

How to keep your healing

Your faith to be healed operates out of your perspective of God's ability to heal. The more you operate out of believing God will heal because of your obedience, the more you will be healed and the level of faith will increase because of what you see God doing. It is more often the case that you will lose your healing because you do not know how to keep it. Since I started instructing people how to keep their healing, I have found an increase in the rate of conditions that remained healed.

Practice how to be fully healed

When you have lived with a condition for an extended amount of time you must be reminded to change how you act and think. Your mind and body must be retrained to change how to do even the simplest things differently than what you have done before. This may seem basic, but it is a very important step to live out your healing. For example, after people are healed I usually have them perform typical activities such as walking, climbing stairs, or sitting and standing, to experience their healing and to practice how to be active in their new physical abilities. It is very common for a person who is healed to continue walking with the same limp or awkward movement as if they still had the condition. At that moment I would have the person practice walking again, but this time we would talk about what it means to walk as if they were well, without the condition. It would take a few trial walks to begin the retraining of the mind and body. Lastly, give the prayee general instructions about keeping their healing.

A woman slowly walked in to see me leaning on her cane for fear of falling. She described an injury that caused her to have two herniated discs and a lumbar fusion with rods, screws, and a cage in the L4 and L5 area. She said there was severe pain at a number eight (zero to ten scale) for ten years with an unsteady walk from her left leg being shorter. She shared her worry that the doctors wanted to repeat another fusion in the lumbar area, which she did not want to have. When I prayed over the left leg God immediately adjusted the legs to become even. As I prayed for God to heal the spine, her pain began to decrease and she sat up straighter. The pain was 80 percent gone. I suggested that she exercise her faith by standing and walking around. Before she stood I instructed her how to remain in her healing by believing and thinking of her healing and not her illness. She stood up and as she walked she noticed the pain became less and less. She had the biggest smile on her face as she began to move more freely by walking faster, then jumping up and down in excitement. She walked out standing straight while she twirled her cane with her fingers because she didn't need to use it. Praise God!

When you are partially healed

There will be situations where you or those you pray for become partially healed. During these times it is imperative that instructions are provided regarding how to keep what has been gained and continue seeking for the rest of what God has for you. After the initial healing, it is much easier to fall out of partial healing because you still have a remnant of the condition which can easily create doubt about your total healing. The key to success is to focus on what God *has* healed and how much the condition has changed rather than what has not changed, and to continue activating your healing by walking, talking, and thinking as if you are healed. It is very common for you to think the prayer did not work if you did not get fully healed so it is important to practice the activities you can now do in your healing. It is important to emphasize scriptures in order to show the promises of God and encourage you to keep your mind focused on your healing.

A man said he had a knotted muscle in his neck that caused an inability to turn his head and a pain at a number eight. He thought it was a strained neck from working out or from emotional tension. After I prayed for God to heal the neck the pain decreased to a number five. When I saw him several days later he told me he went through the week with difficulty to turn his neck and a pain about a number four. He told me a doctor said his condition was caused by a virus that was going around. In the name of Jesus I cut off the spirit of virus and prayed for God's healing and for the muscles to relax. He was able to turn his head more with less pain. I instructed him to believe what we prayed for and that God had healed him. He said those words relaxed him. When he returned home as he was playing with his dog (and not paying attention to his pain level), he suddenly noticed the pain was completely gone with full range of movement in his neck. Praise God!

Keeping Your Healing Instructions

After someone has been healed, one of the ways to keep that healing is to share the following general information.

Encouragement

Even when you experience the joy of healing, you will need a great deal of encouragement to counter any discouragement created when the illness was present. When you have lived a long time with a condition that has impacted your life there is always the feeling (and potentially the spirit) of discouragement. If the prayee speaks negatively over themself and the future of their healing, you should pray against the spirit of discouragement or against whatever words they say.

For example, you may pray:

In the name of Jesus I bind and send away the negative spirit of _____ *and replace it with God's spirit of (the opposite)*. Other encouraging statements you may use are:

God loves you and wants the best for you.

Praise God that you are obedient to trust Him.

You are a child of God and He wants you to experience good things.

Tell others about what God has done. God likes others to know about Him.

Keep up the good work of walking [or whatever has been healed].

Believe and act on your faith

God's obligation is to heal you when you ask for healing. Your obligation is to stand in faith believing you received your healing and act on your faith as if you believe it. Believe your healing by exercising your faith. That is what Jesus wants you to know when he said, ". . . all things for which you pray and ask, believe that you have received them, and they will be *granted* you," (Mark 11:24). This is done by thinking and acting in the belief you have been healed through everything you do. The next two to three weeks may be an adjustment period. You will need to think and act as a healthy person and not as you did as a sick person. (It is recommended not to stop any medication or medical treatment until the doctor is consulted.) For example, if God healed your back or leg, when you stand or walk, focus on walking as a healed person. Walk with normal steps, thinking and believing you are healed, rather than how you lived when you had an illness.

Focus on the healing

Focus on your healing and not on your illness. You can lose your healing if your mind begins to worry or you begin to feel any discomfort. Without knowing it, your mind can become consumed by the discomfort. Once you have experienced small pains or thoughts of the former condition, stay in your healing by rebuking your pain or thoughts and reclaim your belief that you are healed. For example, if you experience a small ache, you can say, "In the name of Jesus I send away this pain. I am healed and I will have nothing to do with this pain. Thank you Jesus for my healing." Then go back to thinking about how God healed you (even if the ache is still there).

Bind the evil one

The devil does not want you to believe in your healing or experience freedom from your healing. It is important that you do what the Bible emphasizes. "Resist the devil and he will flee from you," (James 4:7). Remember that you are really battling more than just a sickness, but a force that doesn't want you healed. However, as a Christian you have been given the authority against the evil one (Col. 2:9-11). So when you pray to send away the pain, you have already been given God's gift of healing and you can tell the enemy to leave and take the pain with him. For example, think of pain in your body as an evil spirit. As a Christian you have the power and authority to send away that spirit in the name of Jesus.

Build your faith

It is hard to muster up the faith for healing if you do not believe in healing before you start praying. If doubt is often on your mind, you will struggle with your faith until you find the origin of that doubt. The well-known healer, Smith Wigglesworth, said many years ago, "If you wait to build your faith till you need it it's too late." Faith is an action word which means it is activated by what you do with your healing. If you do not act on what you can do, you are more likely to lose your faith to do more. It is also important to spend quality time every day in the Bible meditating on the Word of God and attend a Bible study if possible. The more you know what the Word of God says about healing the stronger you will believe in your healing and the more confident you will pray for the healing of others. It would be helpful to attend or visit a church that is a Bible reading, miracle believing, Jesus praising, place of believers that openly experience the Spirit of God. Talk and pray with others about what God is doing regarding your healing experiences. It is important to spend time with like-minded believers that are positive thinkers and will encourage you in your faith. As you continue to step out in faith and look for more opportunities to pray for people, God will reward your faithfulness with greater miracles, ". . . He is a rewarder of those who seek Him" (Hebrews 11:6).

A man named Joe was telling others how he felt the need to pray for a neighbor that had a stroke but he could not get enough nerve to go up to the man. When I heard the story I asked Joe if I could pray with him to declare God's spirit of boldness over him. He agreed and we prayed together. A week later Joe said he prayed one day, "Lord, if you want me to pray for my neighbor make it obvious." Within the next two days Joe was sitting by his front window in view of his front yard. He saw his neighbor taking his daily walk and stopping to take a break leaning against Joe's own mail box just yards from his front door! Joe became so excited that he ran out to greet the neighbor. Joe told the neighbor that he had been meaning to pray for his condition. The neighbor was surprised by the generous request and allowed Joe to pray. As Joe prayed, little happened with his neighbor at that time, instead Joe became healed of his own condition of neuropathy (numbness) and pain in his feet. Joe could not walk barefoot because of the pain, which now was gone! Praise God! I believe God healed Joe as a result of his willingness to step out in faith.

When there is not enough time to give detailed instructions

When you are ministering to someone in a store or on the street corner you may not have much time to give detailed instructions about keeping your healing. During brief healing encounters it is important to give the prayee encouraging words about how much God loves them and wants to see them healed. Sitting with friends at a restaurant waiting for our meals to be served I noticed our waitress limping. The simple thought came across my mind, *pray for her*. When she served our meal I asked if she hurt her leg. She said she injured it and there was a slight pain. I asked if I could pray for her to help the pain. She stood silent. I knew I had to do something since she was put on the spot. I said God loved her and wanted to help the pain by praying for her. She said the pain was at the top of her left foot. Without touching her, I softly prayed a quick prayer out loud asking God to heal the pain and for the spirit of pain to leave. Since I knew she had to go, I asked if she felt any different. She said she would need to walk around and let us know. I told her to believe that God loved her and wanted to show it through what He does. When she came back a while later she said, "You were right, I don't feel anything. That's incredible!" We again told her about God's love for her. Praise God for His healing!

If you have little time, give some type of instructions such as:

Keep believing in what God has done by keeping your mind focused on the healing rather than what you felt before.

You can also mention instructions such as:

Continue to walk, sit, and move your arms [whatever they can do now] *as if you are healed. If you begin to feel any discomfort, say out loud, "Spirit of pain I command you to leave in the name of Jesus. Thank you Jesus for my healing."*

When you do not know if you are healed

When you have a condition that you can see, feel, hear, taste, or smell, you have a tangible way to measure the validity and success of the healing experience. If the prayee has a condition that they cannot see or feel and do not know if it is healed, such as an internal tumor, it can be more difficult to recognize your healing. I have worked with prayees that have felt an overwhelming evidence of healing inside their body and then others that did not feel or sense anything. When you cannot determine any healing you are more susceptible to doubt and waver in your faith. This is the time where the prayee needs a big dose of encouraging words and scriptures that ideally should be written down to be repeatedly referred to in the coming days. Give the prayee brief instruction about keeping their healing and recommend they visit their doctor for any follow up evaluation to determine any changes in their condition.

A man told me he had been evaluated by his doctor for several years regarding his poor memory. His exam results indicated symptoms of Alzheimer's. After we prayed for God to send the symptoms of Alzheimer's out of his life, I told the man to simply believe in his healing. During a doctor's visit a week later the same exam showed a significantly higher score. When the man asked the doctor how he could account for the higher score, the doctor simply said, "It's not Alzheimer's." Praise God!

Chapter 8

Changing the Atmosphere To Believe In Your Healing

CRAIG MILLER

I was asked by the facilitator of a cancer support group to speak at their monthly meeting. While praying about what to say I realized I did not want to give a typical monologue about how to live with cancer. Instead, I wanted to change the way they thought and lived—I did not want to *support* cancer, I wanted to eliminate it. I also knew that I needed to be sensitive to how each person thought, believed, and lived at the various stages of the condition. I realized I needed to change the atmosphere. I needed to think different, believe different, and share examples about living differently to take the listeners to a new plateau of belief. The group members were very receptive to learning how to receive authority over their condition, forgiveness and destiny over their life, and hear healing testimonies to encourage their faith. Lastly, the group repeated a prayer out loud to renounce and send away in the name of Jesus: the diagnosis; word curses; unresolved emotional trauma, and the seed of cancer. Even though no one said they were healed and there was nothing noticeably different, I knew God arranged this meeting so I had to believe that what happened in His name was the best I could do and then give the rest of the healing work to Him. Two weeks later I received an email from the group facilitator, who wrote that all the cancer patients who attended are now, ". . . in remission or are cured!" Even though I did not pray for any individual group member with cancer, I praise God that He can still work through the atmosphere!

Whatever healing prayer setting you are in, whether it is in a church, factory, office, store, home, or on the street, you should be aware of the type of atmosphere in which you are ministering. In essence, your atmosphere includes what is happening around you and more specifically, what you or others believe, think, and act on your belief within that atmosphere. Your ability to take authority over the atmosphere is an essential ingredient that can influence the outcome. Jesus took authority by changing the atmosphere when He asked the mourners to leave the room before He prayed for the dead girl (Mark 5:38-41). Similar to Jesus, for successful prayer, you may find it necessary to change the atmosphere by praying to send away evil spirits, ask people to leave, or move your prayer time to another location.

Building a faith atmosphere

Faith is an active word, which awaits your action for His Glory. Your faith requires that you risk what you cannot do or believe on your own and what you cannot see or feel that is happening in front of you. Faith is about believing that nothing is impossible for God (Luke 1:37) and that God will reward you as you seek the impossible (Hebrews 11:6). As you pray for healing, you will be confronted with doubt and your faith will be tested with thoughts such as, *Is God going to answer my prayer? I've never prayed for a condition like this,* or *this is a severe condition, what if nothing happens?*

The good news is you do not have to worry because healing is God's responsibility. Your job is to pray and then let God do His job to heal. Worrying about what happens after you pray only confirms several things: it's all about you and not about God, your heart and relationship with God needs to be strengthened, and you need to grow in the area of trust and confidence. Building an atmosphere of faith with someone you pray for is about ushering in the presence of God by showing His love and telling about His love.

Showing God's love is demonstrated through active encouragement, active listening, affirming their story, and validating their feelings. This is done in the following ways:

- Active encouragement – initiate words that build up, support, confirm, and encourage

- Active listening - making eye contact when they talk, nod your head showing you understand

- Affirming their story – making affirming comments, e.g., *I really appreciate you telling me that, sounds like you went through a very difficult time*

- Validating their feelings – repeat back the feelings you hear

Telling about God's love will draw people toward God and bring a desire for what God has to offer. This can easily be done by telling people how much God loves them before and after the prayer, no matter what happens. Share testimonies of other healings and share encouraging scriptures or healing testimonies from your life and from the Bible.

- Some healing scriptures include: Mathew 21:22; John 14:12-14; Luke 1:37; Luke 4:18; I Peter 2:24; James 5:14-15.

- Some Bible healing testimonies include: Matthew 8:2-4; Matthew 9:20-22; Mark 2:3-12; Mark 8:22-26; Luke 11:14; John 9:1-7

I was talking to a woman who had been depressed for many years who asked me why I wanted to help someone like her. As I looked at her with compassion I said, "Because you are a wonderful child of God." Her eyes teared up as she asked, "How can someone you can't see, like God, love you more than your parents?"

When I asked what she meant by that she explained that her parents were not emotionally there for her when she was a child. She recalled that when she tried to get close to her father, her mother would become jealous and say or do hurtful things. I acknowledged her story and validated her feelings by commenting how sad and lonely that must have been when she did not receive love from either parent. Realizing the sad truth of not being loved by her parents, she acknowledged that her current feelings of despair and emptiness were the same unresolved emotions of her childhood. I asked if she wanted to release those hurtful emotions and experience God's love. When she said, "Yes," I asked the woman to think of Jesus with the lonely, hurting little girl. I had her imagine Jesus putting His arm around her and giving His love. I put my hand on her head and prayed the Father's love to be poured over her. She began to cry and sobbed for some time. When she stopped crying I asked what was going on inside. She said she felt the joy of God's love in her heart for the first time in her life. Praise God!

Taking authority

Your words and thoughts are powerful. When someone gives you a negative word or a medical diagnosis, especially someone in authority, the power of the tongue can bring you death or life (Proverbs 18:21). What you are told can determine what you believe and becomes the foundation from which you live. Proverbs 23:7 states, "For as he thinketh within himself, so is he." When you believe a negative word about your life, those words can literally hijack your identity and drag the health and life right out of you. Consequently, the more you live and talk about the condition in every area of your life, the more your identity becomes entrenched in that condition. For example, every time you say, "I am diagnosed with _____," or "I have arthritis," or "my cancer," you are allowing the condition to take ownership, power, and control over your life to do whatever it wants.

A woman was diagnosed with Scoliosis five years earlier with very re-stricted movement in her body for the past two years. I put my hands on her back and asked God to cut off the diagnosis of Scoliosis, command-ing Scoliosis condition to leave and heal the vertebra to become straight with a normal alignment in the body. In Jesus name I commanded any pain to leave and the muscle, tendons, and ligaments to become relaxed and free to move. The pain disappeared. When I instructed the woman to do something she could not do before, she twisted, turned, and bent over to touch her toes. She was completely healed! Praise God!

Whenever you step into a ministry situation, as a Christian you are an ambassador of Christ and as a healer you have the authority and power of Christ. When you pray, you activate your faith and change the atmosphere for what Christ can do as you ask for it. You should first be aware of the overall atmosphere setting to where you are praying. If you have the time, you may want to observe what is in the room, who is in the room, and other potential distractions that may arise before you pray.

I realize that God can overcome any obstacle and your love and faith can move you through many issues. However, the more aware you are of the influences the less potential hindrances you may encounter. Next, be aware of how rooted the condition may be by listening and observing what is said and done. This will give a better indication of what you are working with and how you can pray.

Helpful suggestions when taking authority

- Stop referring to the condition with ownership words such as, "My," "I have," or "I am."
- Denounce whatever words or diagnosis that were made over your life. *In the name of Jesus I denounce and send out of my life the diagnosis of _____ and I ask my heavenly Father to replace those words with the Spirit of life and wellness.*
- Forgive the people who said the words or diagnosis over you.
- Forgive yourself for accepting and believing those words or diagnosis.
- Identify any feelings as a result of the condition, e.g., hurt, anger, sadness.
- If you have time, use the technique, Heart Transformation for Emotional Healing.
- If you do not have time, do the following: think of the condition in your body, picture yourself handing the condition to Jesus, and ask Jesus and yourself for forgiveness for holding on to the condition

Confronting the darkness

When you confront the darkness with the Light, you are contending for the present stronghold territory (2 Corinthians 10:3-4). The good news is you do not have to battle with the enemy because the healing territory belongs to God anyway and the evil is illegally trespassing in that territory. You just need to take authority, bind the stronghold, and claim the healing in the name of Jesus. Whatever you bind on earth will be bound in heaven, and whatever you loose on earth will be loosed in heaven (Matthew 16:19). Among the reasons why demonic activity remains in the atmosphere is because you give it authority by either not realizing it as evil or you become afraid and do nothing about it. When I was traveling to a European country as a Global Awakening team member I remember the first night of prayer at a church in England where I felt a heaviness and prayers did not bring results as you would expect. Later that night when the Global Awakening team members talked, I found everyone had similar struggles. We concluded there was a stronghold in the church that hindered our prayers which needed to be sent away. The next morning the team prayed to bind any strongholds of evil within the church and among the people entering the church. The prayer time that night was very different. Everyone experienced a stronger presence of God resulting in amazing physical and emotional healings.

The enemy does not want you to be victorious with healing prayer and can go to any length to create a diversion in the atmosphere before or during prayer to keep you or the prayee distracted from experiencing what God has for you. Any one of the following suggested distractions can hinder healing prayer either by affecting the prayee or the prayer minster (see the previous chapter on Spiritual Warfare hindering prayer for more details regarding individual warfare).

- Sudden change in room temperature
- Sense of heaviness, gloom, or darkness in the room
- Seeing dark shadows
- More than usual interruptions from people, cell phones, or other noises
- Any out of the ordinary interruptions or disturbances

Suggested prayer

There is no specific formula on how to take your rightful authority against any evil in the atmosphere. Primarily you are to bind and send away in the name of Jesus whatever you sense needs to be cleared from the atmosphere and replace it with whatever is good. For example, *In the name of Jesus, I bind and send away any demonic strongholds of the enemy and replace it with God's love and healing power.*

There are different opinions regarding the presence or existence of evil spirits lingering in the atmosphere. The bottom line is that evil spirits are real; they can remain in the atmosphere unless they are told to leave, they are under the authority of Jesus Christ and under the command of a Christ filled believer who speaks in the name of Jesus. A mother was receiving guidance to deal with her rebellious and uncooperative teenage son. Overall there was a mutual loving relationship and the son was medically healthy and typically cooperative. However, the mother was baffled as to why the son had these periods of rebellion. It was discovered that these rebellion times were often when the boy wore a sweatshirt, given to him by a friend, which had a large skull and cross bones pictured on it. When the mother got rid of the sweatshirt, the boy's attitude suddenly improved and the rebellion stopped. You cannot ignore that we are living in a spiritual world where good and bad spirits exist. You have the power to determine how the spirits will affect your life.

In another case, a mother complained of her four-year-old daughter who was rebellious and acted very oddly in the basement of their home but not anywhere else. The mother said she searched throughout the basement and could not find anything unusual. When the mother was asked to look again, she found a stack of pornographic material that had been hidden away. When the mother removed the inappropriate material, the odd and rebellious behavior completely stopped. It is important to consider evil spirits as a potential cause. Most importantly, you do not need to be afraid of evil spirits as long as you are a spirit filled Christian that loves the Lord. You have more authority than the evil in the world (John 10:9-10). If you do not feel comfortable with praying for someone with potential spiritual warfare issues, be wise and refer the person to someone that is more qualified.

Creating an atmosphere of encouragement out of discouragement

When healing doesn't happen, it is important to know how to transition an attitude of disappointment to an atmosphere of encouragement. Disappointment means you are focused on yourself and not on what God is doing. God is still in the healing business and in control of the situation even if you do not see it or feel it. If healing doesn't happen, do not allow discouragement to rule the atmosphere. Change the atmosphere and speak life and wellness into the prayee and situation. You must not fall into the belief that the healing opportunity is over because healing did not happen at that moment. You still have the greatest chance to bring healing through the words and attitude you impart during that short window of time. Your words are extremely powerful and can change the destiny of the person you pray for no matter the circumstances.

During a session break at a conference I noticed a woman wearing a knee brace and walking very carefully. When I asked about her knee she said the ACL and meniscus were torn and she was going to have surgery in two days. She was in pain and had to walk very slowly. She was very receptive to prayer, so her friend (a pastor's wife) and I prayed. I prayed five different times for God's healing in every possible way I could think, with no change in her knee condition. Since I had to get back to speaking, I showered her with praise, encouragement and instruction to believe in the promises of God. I said, "Since God loves you and we asked for His healing, He wants to give you what you desire for His glory." I went back to the podium and she hobbled back to her chair. Many weeks later I received an email telling me the rest of the story. Two days after the conference when she went for surgery, the doctor took an X-ray. Upon reviewing the X-ray they could not find any problems with her knee and cancelled the surgery. All the doctor said was, "There must have been some mistake with the first X-ray." However, we knew the truth. Praise God!

If healing does not happen, and you detect there is more emotional or physical *baggage* than you either have time or expertise for, I recommend you gently ask if they have ever talked to anyone about their emotions regarding their condition. I believe that anyone you minister to is an assignment from God and you have a God-opportunity to speak into that person's life. It may be the only opportunity for the person to hear the truth and for all you know, it may be the last opportunity of their life. Take that God-opportunity to help each person out of a life of hurt and destruction into a life of healing and wellness. If you see emotional, social, physical, or moral issues that may be hindering healing, gently mention that there may be other issues interfering with their health that need to be taken care of. If they ask what that may be, gently share your thoughts. Otherwise, gently mention they may benefit from additional counseling for other underlying issues affecting their healing.

At a healing conference a man and wife came to me for healing prayer. The man had surgery a year earlier for a brain tumor. As a result of the surgery he lost sight in one eye, partial loss of sight in the other, and had problems with his thinking. As a result, he lost his job and had to be assisted by his wife for everything. I could see the desperation in their eyes and exhaustion on their faces. At the time, I felt confident that God was going heal this man. Even though I asked all the right questions and prayed for God's healing the best way I could, there was no change in the condition. As I looked at their faces, I was concerned about them falling deeper into doubt and despair, so I realized the extreme importance that I stay focused on what God can do and not let myself fall into discouragement too. At that moment, God reminded me that I still had the greatest opportunity to speak into this man what God can do by bringing healing through his heart (rather than his body). I told the man a testimony of how God still heals. I told him to never stop seeking what is getting in the way of his right to be healed and seeking the very healing that God has for him. They did not see the healing at that moment, but they left with a different belief that opened him up for his future healing. I'll admit that I had some struggle with discouragement at first, but I realized God wanted me to look beyond what was happening to help the couple change their view of God and their healing.

The next night when I was praying again, the wife came to me alone for prayer. Interestingly, she could have stood in line with any other prayer team member, but she came to see me for prayer regarding her feelings of being lost and sad about life. As I prayed, God was faithful and released her from her life of despair. I believe that God used the situation with her husband the previous night to open the opportunity to bring the wife out of her despair and into a different place emotionally and spiritually—in order to bring her into healing and help support her husband into his healing.

Helpful suggestions to create encouragement out of discouragement

- Speak encouraging, uplifting words to build a future and a hope.
- Share similar healing testimonies.
- Say and write down encouraging scriptures and words of Jesus.
- Stand on the promise God loves them and wants to give what you asked.
- Connect with other Christians for continuing prayer.
- Encourage counseling to deal with underlying emotional issues.

Chapter 9
Maintain Your Power And Authority
CRAIG MILLER

Many years ago I remember counseling with a woman where all of a sudden she started hissing and yelling, which caught me by surprise and created a streak of fear up my spine. I immediately sensed something not of God and felt choked up, feeling as if I couldn't speak for a moment. After taking authority over the situation in the name of Jesus and commanding the spirit to leave, the woman calmed down and became free of the spirit. As I drove home after work I had a feeling of heaviness in my mind and body, which at the time I simply believed it was a typical reaction from a long day of counseling people. When I climbed into bed to sleep I could not rest. My mind seemed confused, whirling (more than usual!) and the same feeling of heaviness I felt earlier seemed to be stronger than usual. I knew there was something wrong with how I felt, and I knew it was not from God. I got out of bed and walked into the garage so I would not disturb my sleeping family. Out loud I commanded any evil spirit to leave my mind and body in the name of Jesus. As I prayed I felt a feeling of gloom and fuzzy thinking immediately leave, like something rushed out of my body. I knew I was free, and I was then able to return to bed and fall asleep.

That experience taught me a few valuable lessons about ministering to others—that you can be vulnerable in any ministering situation. No matter what people want to tell you, spirits can transfer to you if you leave yourself unprotected. After you minister with anyone (emotional, physical, or spiritual healing) you should spiritually cleanse yourself and the area you minister in (this is especially important if you pray with people in your own home). You do not want to take any chances that what one person released has any effect on you. A simple prayer such as the following will be helpful.

In the name of Jesus, I send away any evil spirits or anything that does not belong to me or in this room, I command it to leave. Thank you heavenly Father for covering myself, my family, and this room with the blood of Jesus Christ of Nazareth.

You may be thinking, *I don't have to worry about transfer of spirits, that's only when you deal with evil spirits.* I thought that too until experiences showed me otherwise. For example, after an emotional and physical healing conference, one of my ministry team members commented about an ache in her side which started just after our ministry time that night. In our debriefing time after the night session we forgot to address the ache she had. During our prayer time before the conference started the next day, the same team member mentioned about the ache in her back that was still bothering her since the night before. We immediately prayed for God to release any spirits that may have attached to her the night before. At that moment the ache disappeared and never returned. When ministering to others you need to take adequate care of yourself to maintain your God-given authority and power. The following are important ways to care for yourself emotionally, physically, and spiritually.

- Pray and praise before your session (Psalm 7:17; 9:11; 34:1-3, 145:18).
- Prayer coverage increases the power and authority of the Holy Spirit, binds the enemy, and pleases the Lord. (Psalm 145:18; James 5:16).
- Pray over yourself (or have others pray) after the session to release any unwelcome spirits.
- Set aside daily time for personal prayer, devotions, and studying the Word of God.
- Ask others to pray for Holy Spirit guidance and protection.

Enough for others and enough for yourself

If you minister to others do you routinely have the strength to give to others with enough for yourself and your family? The simple fact that you are giving of yourself to others is usually the confirmation you are more of a giver and most likely giving out more than you receive. Helping others is a good trait to possess and very much needed to care for others. However, it only remains a good trait until you do not have enough left to give to yourself or to your own family. When you are taking care of yourself and fill yourself with God, that is when you have more than enough to give your best and have enough for others. Paul writes in 1 Timothy 4:16 for us to "Pay close attention to yourself and to your teaching; persevere in these things, for as you do this you will ensure salvation both for yourself and for those who hear you." Find an opportunity for a prayer minister or elder to pray and minister to you to *ensure* you are having enough for others.

In your need to care for others you may make everyone else number one instead of watching over yourself. If you provide ministry to many people (your flock), the biggest mistake is you make your flock number one. Paul writes in Acts 20:28 that you need to, "Keep watch over yourselves and all the flock of which the Holy Spirit has made you overseers." Who is your flock, your clients, patients, co-workers, parishioners, ministry group, friends, family or potentially anyone you minister with? Regardless, who it is, Paul tells you to first watch out for yourself. You may say, *But how do I watch out for myself and give as Christ gave of Himself?* The best way to find that out is to read some of the following examples of Jesus.

Setting boundaries with others

Jesus was wise enough to know His limits as a caregiver and secure enough in His relationship with the heavenly Father to where He knew when to set boundaries with others and not worry about hurting their feelings. You may think, *But people didn't get hurt back then because they were talking to the Son of God.* Many of the examples of when Jesus interacted with people are when people only knew Him as a man, rabbi, or miracle worker, and did not know Him yet as the Son of God. As His ministry grew, people would demand more of Him and setting boundaries became more of a necessity for Jesus. One example is found in Luke 5:16 that states, "The news about Him spread- so crowds of people came to hear him and to be healed of their sicknesses. But Jesus often withdrew to lonely places and prayed." Another translation states, "He often slipped away to the wilderness and prayed." It would seem Jesus did not let others take advantage of his time with God. He understood that He must set limits with His activities to rejuvenate His spirit with the heavenly Father.

If Jesus could set limits for His own needs, I believe God would expect you to do the same for yourself and your family.

Saying "No" to others

One of the most difficult words for a classic altruistic or rescuing personality trait is to say the word, "No." You may be like so many other prayer ministers, caretakers, and helping professionals where you have difficulty saying, "No," out of a need to fix and rescue others, fear disappointing others, fear of failing as a Christian, or out of obligation and duty. What often starts as a place of compassion can become exhausting, never ending and demanding on the way to becoming purely burnt out. I believe Jesus understood the reason for setting personal boundaries in the example Luke 4:42-43, "At daybreak Jesus went out to a solitary place. The people looked for Jesus- when they found him they tried to keep him from leaving. Jesus said, I must preach the Good News of the kingdom of God to the other towns also, because that is why I was sent." Jesus again did not let others take advantage of His personal time and ministry. In a polite way he was able to say, "No" to the demands of others.

Not being offended by others

One of the most common difficulties of good hearted, compassionate givers is when you become offended, hurt, rejected, slighted, and snubbed by well meaning (and not so well meaning) people that you are trying to help. Unfortunately, churches are full of people that are rejected, dejected, and hurtful. You need to realize that Jesus was rejected, dejected, hurt, and even died because of *religious* people. Your job is not to let others determine and control your thoughts and behaviors but rather let your thoughts and behaviors be controlled by God to determine what you do with others. Jesus knew that not everyone will want to listen or respond to what He said or did as He instructed the disciples in Matthew 10:14

when He said, "If anyone will not welcome you or listen to your words, shake the dust off your feet when you leave that home or town." In the past, I would become disappointed or hurt if people rejected my request to pray for healing. However, I now realize not everyone will be accepting of what I have to give. Instead, I see what I do for Christ as planting a seed so God can nurture it for future growth.

What is hindering you from believing the impossible?

Everyone questions in their head some time or another whether God is going to heal someone (if they tell you different, they are not telling the truth!). With our finite minds it is normal to wonder if the impossible will become possible, but with God nothing is impossible (Luke 1:37). I remember my wife and I were ministering at a church when a ten year old boy came up to me asking for prayer. He told me he was born with club feet, curvature of the spine, and one leg was an inch shorter. He walked and ran with a limp and could not twist his body, bend over, or run without difficulty and had pain in his back and ankles. He had suffered with this his whole life! Although my heart went out to him, I could see he had more faith in me than I had in myself to heal everything he lived with. When he sat down I held his legs and just prayed for God to heal him. Immediately his legs became even, his spine straighten, and the pain vanished. We prayed again and his foot became straighter, with no pain in his ankles. He ran back and forth across the room, twisted his body back and forth, and bent over touching his toes—there was no pain and he was the happiest boy in that room! We gave God all the glory. Praise God!

When I ask someone if they want to help pray to heal the sick, I often receive a hesitant response such as, "I don't have the ability to heal anyone." I tell them, "You're right, you don't have the ability, but Jesus does because He is the one doing the healing!" If you have frequent hesitation, questioning, or doubt when healing opportunities come your way, I recommend the following suggestions:

1. Renew your heart and mind

What you believe and feel can determine how you minister to others and respond to personal healing. When you pray for others, it can be normal to have some questions whether God will bring healing. However, if you frequently doubt, question, wonder, or struggle with healing prayer, you have something(s) hindering your ability to believe in what God can do through you. You need to renew your heart and mind. You need to take time to change what is in your heart (Luke 12:34) and what you believe (Proverbs 23:7). Review the hindrances to healing in this book and determine if there is any belief, emotion, sin, or issue in your life that may need to be resolved and healed. The bottom line is if you want to see God work, get closer to Jesus and meditate on the promises of His Word.

For example:

• If you struggle with doubt, unbelief, and wonder if you are good enough to pray for healing, ask God to find where and when you stopped believing and reveal who or what affected how you believe. Ask God if you have a hardened heart from unresolved hurts and unforgiveness from people who abused you, left you (or died), ridiculed (made fun of) you, or did not provide love and attention. Seek healing of your heart and mind. Spend time with God and ask for His love, attention, boldness, and confidence. I recommend you seek professional Christian counseling if this is a persistent issue in your life.

• If you struggle with fear and question when you pray, ask God to find where and when you stopped feeling safe and reveal who or what affected how safe you feel. Ask God to reveal fearful, abusive, or traumatic circumstances in your life that may have affected how you feel now.

Spend time with God and ask for His peace and love in your heart. I recommend you seek professional Christian counseling if this is a persistent issue in your life.

2. To grow in your faith pray for opportunities beyond what you know and do

Moving beyond your comfort zone is what activates your faith toward the impossible. When you pursue after God, He will reward your faithfulness (Hebrews 11:6). The more you see God work the more you will be encouraged to want more of what God can do. On the way to a town wide street festival my wife and I prayed our typical prayer to have God highlight someone that could use a healing touch. No sooner did we get to the first row of arts and craft booths did we see a woman sitting in her both with a walker next to her. In my excitement I made a comment to her about her walker and asked what condition she had. The woman told her story about difficulty walking from pain in her back. When she let us pray for God to bring healing, her pain disappeared! She was so excited, she asked us to meet her friend in the next both. We found her friend with a cane next to her. We prayed for her and she got healed to! It is fun to ask for healing opportunities. Praise God!

3. Know your authority in Christ

Since you have the same power and authority as Christ, and God is a loving Father who respects each of us the same, what stops you from using God's authority? One of the biggest stumbling blocks to healing is the difficulty in believing and maintaining the authority you have through Jesus Christ. I like to have people learn how to take authority over their own condition and experience the authoritative power they have through Jesus Christ. There was a woman who had right arm pain at number five (zero to ten scale) from the wrist to the elbow from repetitive motion after working on an assembly line. She could not move her arm without severe pain and was unable to close her fingers or grip objects with that hand. After she was able to forgive herself and forgive the company she worked for, we prayed for Jesus to send away the pain. The pain immediately decreased to number four. I wanted her to learn how to take control of her condition, so I asked, "How about you asking Jesus to send away the pain?" After a brief instruction, the moment she asked Jesus to send away the pain, it decreased to number two. We praised God and she commanded the pain to leave again. And the pain was completely gone. Praise God!

As a Christian it is important to remember that you are blessed by God your heavenly Father, who has blessed you with every spiritual blessing in the heavenly places in Christ (Ephesians 1:3). Because of His blessing you have the ability to love and heal others in His name. If you have ever been assigned the responsibility to perform an important task or manage other people, but not given the proper authority, you know how difficult it is to carry out your responsibilities. You find out quickly that you cannot tell others what to do unless you have the proper authority. Similarly, God is extremely aware of what you need to perform what He expects.

God gives you responsibility to:

• Go therefore and make disciples of all the nations, baptizing them in the name of the Father and the Son and the Holy Spirit— Matthew 28:19

• Heal the sick, raise the dead, cleanse the lepers, cast out demons— Matthew 10:8

• Lay hands on the sick, so they will recover—Mark 16:18

God also gives authority:

• Authority over unclean spirits, to cast them out, and to heal every kind of disease and every kind of sickness—Matthew 10:1

• Authority over power of the enemy, nothing can injury you in the spirit realm—Luke 10:19

The most important part is to remember that healing is up to God. You are just the vehicle to make it happen. Your ability to heal is not based on what you can do, but what God can do through your abilities. It is up to you to allow God to work through your abilities to experience what He can do. You just have to do your part to pray and believe in His promises and God will do His part. The good news is that since you cannot take the Glory when the healing happens, you cannot take the disappointment when the healing doesn't happen. It all belongs to God.

Chapter 10
Suggested Meaning of Body Language
CRAIG MILLER

There was a woman that said she wanted healing, but her body showed something different. She sat in front of me with her arms folded and legs crossed. When I prayed for her and there was no change in her condition, it was obvious she was resistant to opening herself to allowing anyone into her life. When I asked if she believed in her healing, she looked surprised at my question, but admitted to having difficulty believing God was there for her. When I asked her about the disappointments in her life that closed her down emotionally, that was when the flood gates opened with tears and the healing was able to begin. The closed body language was a strong indicator of what was happening in her heart. When you are praying for someone, watching the body language before and during the prayer time can be helpful to successful prayer. The following are suggested meanings to body language.

BODY AREA OR GESTURE	SUGGESTED MEANING
Eye lids flutter	Holy Spirit doing something, medical condition
Eyes move rapidly back and forth	Processing information, seeing images
Face or Wrinkle on forehead	Worried, afraid, disappointed, don't know what will happen
Arms crossed	Protective posture, can't let you in, holding in thoughts and feelings, afraid, closed, relaxed
Sitting with legs crossed over knee	Don't want to move forward, protective, sexual issues, setting boundaries, relaxed
Sitting with ankles crossed	Defensiveness, suppressed negative emotion, relaxed
No tears	Shut off, hurt beyond understanding, do not want to be vulnerable, closed, can't show weakness, need to be strong
Sitting farthest away	Afraid to get close, afraid what will happen, unable to trust, setting boundaries

Leaning forward	I want more, I am receptive, I am eager to move forward
Foot tapping	Energy, nervous, wants to move forward but can't, something is holding me back, excited, impatient
Rubbing face	Overwhelmed, trying to relieve feelings
Hands over face	Sadness, hiding, embarrassed, overwhelmed, afraid to be vulnerable, hard time releasing
Staring at floor	Processing information, figuring it out, unsure what to do
Look to upper right	Creating images, imagination
Look to upper left	Recalling images, accessing memories
Looking to lower left	Thinking through things, trying to work it out, picturing an image
Looking to lower right	Questioning their feelings, trying to figure out how they feel
Rubbing eyes	Sad, upset, disbelief, tired
Shaking	Medical or neurological condition, God or evil spirit manifesting

Chapter 11
Suggested Emotional Connection to Mind/Body Conditions
CRAIG MILLER

How to use this information for healing:

- Find the condition and read over the suggested emotional issues with that condition

- Pray for guidance to identify in your life when you experienced the suggested emotions

- Use the Heart Transformation for Emotional Healing technique for healing (See Pages 95-98)

Abasia:
Difficulty "thinking straight"
Easily distracted, afraid of things not working out

Abdominal Area:
Incorrect use of judgment (wisdom)
Identifies with possessions, little sense of self
Feeling possessive of someone
Worrying about others
Feeling undue tension, fear and anxiety which constricts the energy flow
Disharmony and bondage in relationships
Bound up in present fears and not trusting

Abdominal Cramps:
Distrust, stuck, feeling tension
Afraid of what will happen
Feels responsible for giving understanding
Grew up in dysfunctional family
Struggle with moving forward

Abscesses:
Seething; unresolved hurt feelings
Wanting revenge

Acid Reflux:
Fear of abandonment
Feel restricted, hold in feelings
Fear of things happening

Addictions:
Unable to perceive clearly and correctly
Disapproval of self/running from self
Feelings of self-rejection, despair
Feeling a void in the soul, avoids feeling
Feel unloved, rarely satisfied, impulsive

Addison's Disease:
Lacks understanding of self/no sense of self
Anger at the self
Inability to understand own emotions
Feels no mercy for self

Adenoids:
Acute disharmony in the home
Feels restricted in life/in breathing

Child feels unacceptance or hostility from someone
Feels unwelcome, in the way

Adrenal Problems:
Feels like a *victim*
Feelings of being defective
"Don't care what happens to me"
Feelings of anxiety
Misusing the will
Subconscious belief that life must have burdens
Unresolved jealousies and fears
Must struggle for success, power or position

AIDS:
Feeling defenseless and hopeless
Feels nobody cares
Belief of "not good enough"
Denial of the self
Extreme deep-rooted anger

Alcoholism:
Inability to cope/futility/"What's the use?" attitude
Feelings of worthlessness/self-rejection
Feelings of living a lie/guilt/inadequacy
Locked in by unresolved negative emotions
Locked in by believing the negative words of others
Protecting against feelings one is afraid to feel

Allergies:
Suppressed weeping
Imitation substitute for colds
Don't have an answer to change
Fear of sharing feelings
Stifled, denying own power

Alzheimer's Disease:
Tired of coping
Can't face life anymore
Unable to be in control of life
Inferiority and insecurity
Suppressed anger
Wants to live in own little world
Hopelessness and helplessness

Anemia:
Angry at self for inability to control things
Feeling life is not going the way I want

Feelings of "I'm not enough"
Manipulative but resentful at being manipulated
Feels there is no joy
Lack of order in life

Anemia: (Pernicious)
Feelings of total helplessness
Have given up
Deep, unresolved grief

Ankles:
Fears falling or failing, inflexibility
Instability in present situation

Ankles: (Swollen)
Feeling overworked, but can't quit
Feels there is no relief from pressures in life

Anorectal Bleeding:
Anger and frustration

Anorexia:
Unable to please parent (usually mother)
Unable to live up to expectations of others
Self-rejection/self-hatred

Anxiety:
(Also see Panic Attacks, Separation Anxiety)
Unable to "call the shots" in life
Helpless to affect change
Cannot change my situation, no control
Past trauma unresolved

Apathy:
"Spark of life" has been turned off
Doesn't want to feel

Appendicitis:
Undue fears about life
Unable to deal with fear; energy flow is restricted

Appetite:
(Loss of) Incorrect perceptions causing distrust and a form of depression
(Excessive) Feeding the need for love, acceptance and protection

Arteriosclerosis:
Inability to express feelings
Unable to see the good
Unresolved feelings inside
Refusing to be open-minded

Arthritis:
Criticizing self or others
Holding on to hostility
Holding on to beliefs
Long term tension or anger
Anxiety and/or depression over long periods
Belief it's wrong to get angry
Repressed anger that *eats you up*
Needs to be *right*
Rigid in thinking and feelings
Uncompromising attitude
Inflexibility

Arthritis – Rheumatoid:
Body receiving conflicting messages,
Laughing on outside, crying on inside
Feels helpless to change life's burdens

Asthma:
Reliving childhood fears
Need for dependence
Chronic anxiety and fear
Unconscious dependency wishes
Feeling dominated by a parent
Wanting to protest, but unable
Being over-sensitive
Suppressed sorrow or crying
Feelings of being stifled

Attachment Difficulties:
Issues of abandonment
Afraid to get hurt, cannot trust
Afraid you will leave me
Afraid to be alone, fear of loss
Hurt by important people
Important people not there for me
Past trauma unresolved

Autoimmune System:
Laughing on the outside, but crying on the inside
Feels totally helpless

Have given up
Deep seeded/seated grief

Back Problems:
Feeling no support
Can't cope with emotional difficulties
Feeling burdened emotionally
Feelings of frustration
Wanting someone to "get off my back"

Back – Upper:
Feels unsupported or burdened emotionally
Withholding your love from others
Feeling agitated or anxious
Feelings of frustration

Back – Middle:
Feeling guilty
Lacking self-support and self-confidence

Back – Lower:
Feels unsupported financially
Experiencing fear where money is concerned
Wanting to back out of something
In a relationship that hurts
Running away from a situation

Bedwetting:
Feeling fear, rejection, unworthy, anger
Unable to control situation
Anxiety, distrust of self and others

Bladder Problems:
Fear, peeved, stifled, pissed, timid, inefficient, need for approval, feels out of control, feels ineffective, weary/tired,
Repressing of sexual feelings
Inharmonious male and female emotional relationships
Sexual identity going unexpressed
Unable to release things
Feels over concerned with survival issues (money, job, health)
Lack of order or obsessed with order

Bleeding Gums:
Inability to feel joy over decisions

Blisters:
Feeling unprotected emotionally
Resisting flow of life, unsafe

Blood Disorders:
Feeling powerless in some area of life
Feelings of deep anger
Feelings of long-standing ill will
Intense depression

Blood Problems:
Not feeling joy in life
Stagnant thinking
Unable to flow with life
Feelings of fear

Blood Pressure – High:
Feeling pressured, endangered
Powerless, hold in feelings
Overly self reliant, cannot relax

Blood Pressure – Low:
Feeling defeated, resentment
Feeling unloved, anxiety, unsafe

Bones: (Broken)
Feelings of separation
The feeling nature is very obstinate or fixed

Bowels:
Fear of displeasing a loved one
Fear of releasing the old that is no longer useful
Fearful of not having ample means
Unable to control outer situation
Tries to control a situation
Unwillingness to relinquish control
Inability to eliminate possessive attitudes

Bronchitis:
Extreme disharmony in the home
Angry, hold it in, afraid to let it out
Fear, tension, anxiety, helpless

Bulimia:
Mistaken self-image
Inability to accept self
Feelings of no control over one's self

Unsatisfied needs never met
Feelings of self-contempt
Feels unable to measure up to others expectations

Bunions:
Constant and chronic fear

Bursitis:
Anxiety, repressed anger
Feel you have *lost control*
Feeling helpless to change a situation
Tension built up
Holding back hitting someone
Frustrated with the flow of life

Calluses:
Inability to flow with life
Not wanting to circulate
Not open to new learning

Cancer:
Of blood – Leukemia:
Intense depression, anger or ill will

Of cervix:
Repressed anger

Of female organs:
Repressed anger (usually at male authority figures)
Feeling an emptiness in life
Unresolved resentments
Feelings of hostility being suppressed
Rejecting the self
Feelings of despair
Feelings of loneliness being repressed
Poor relationship with parents
Inability to cope with a traumatic loss
Feelings of hopelessness/helplessness being repressed
Mental depression
Holding on to deep anger, resentment, hate, revenge or jealousy
Not open to "light" or divine help
Sub-conscious death with – no desire to live

Of small of back:
Continual inside strife, but appearing happy
Carrying life's burdens
Unresolved emotional burdens

<u>Of stomach:</u>
Feelings of condemnation and hatred
Feelings of malice and wanting to *get even*
Unforgiveness

Candida:
Resentment multiplying inside
Inability to claim one's own power
Unresolved negative feelings molding in the body
Blames others on sub-conscious level

Canker Sores:
Unresolved negativity
Overwork coupled with emotional stress
Emotional upset and anxious over details

Cataracts:
Feeling gloomy/afraid of future
Cannot control life or future, helpless
Avoids looking to future

Carpel Tunnel:
Feeling that life isn't fair
Inability to claim one's own power
Feeling justice is never served in your behalf

Cardiovascular Disorder:
Driven to compete, achieve and material wealth
Feelings of agitation and impatience
Wanting matters to move more quickly
Low self-esteem

Cerebral Palsy:
Feeling stuck in thought and life
Must make everything right
Too responsible, guilty, rejection
Difficulty letting go or forgiving

Chest:
Belief and emotional center of life
Unidentified unresolved fears
Not feeling approval, lack of self love
Inability to claim one's own power
Feelings of being unprotected
Hurts where love in concerned

Cholesterol:
Belief that "I'm not supposed to be happy"
Denying self joy

Chronic Diseases:
Distrusts the process of life
Unwilling to change for the better
Feel unsafe, do not take chances

Chronic Fatigue Syndrome:
Feelings of despair, desolation
Feeling totally alone
Feeling "It's no use" (hopelessness)
No will to live, low self-worth

Circulation Problems:
Feeling overloaded
Not enjoying job, but can't quit or let go
Feelings of tension and discouragement
Feeling "I must prove myself, but how?"

Colds:
Unkind feelings toward someone
Confusion in the home
Confusion in life
Belief in seasonal sickness

Cold Sores: (Fever Blisters)
Inability to express anger
Feeling pressured or burdened by responsibilities
Unable to cope with pressures of life
Feeling resentful of the load you are carrying

Colic:
Not happy with surroundings
Feelings of irritation and impatience

Colitis:
Overly concerned with order (lose freedom)
Worrying excessively
Feelings of oppression and defeat
Feel a need for more affection

Colitis – Ulcerative:
In people with obsessive-compulsive behavior
Indecisiveness

Feelings of anxiety
Unable to express hostility or anger
Feels a need to conform, like a martyr

Colon Problems:
Difficulty processing and handling issues
Hard to let go and hold on to past
Unresolved hurts caught up with them

Conjunctivitis:
Feelings of frustration at what you see in life
Feelings of anger towards life
Not seeing the perfection in people and life

Congestive Heart Failure:
Rejection, abandonment, unloved
No one there for you, hopeless
Broken heart issues from past

Constipation:
Constantly fretting and anxious
Unwilling to release old feelings and beliefs
Resisting the flow of life
Unresolvable problems/determined to carry on

Corns:
Holding on to hurts of the past
Hardened feelings

Coughs:
Nervousness, holding in negative thoughts
Feelings of criticism and annoyance
Feel like you're choking on life

Cramps:
Fear of pain
Holding on to incorrect perceptions of femininity
Tension built up

Cysts:
Feeling sorry for self
Inability resolve hurt feelings

Cystic Fibrosis:
Belief that "life works for everyone but me"
Chronic grief, depression, joy-avoidant
Unworthy of living a full life

Cystitis:
Unresolved irritability
Habitual unhappy thought patterns

Deafness:
Not wanting to hear what is going on
Lack of self-love
Feeling of poor self-worth
Wanting to be isolated
Feels more comfortable in own little world

Defiant Behaviors/Thinking:
Unloved, abandoned, betrayed
Rejected, neglected, not special
Important people not there for me
Others get more attention than me
If I misbehave I will get more attention

Dementia:
Feeling hopeless and helpless
Tired of having to struggle with life
Unresolved anger

Depression:
Do not care about life, discouraged
Feelings of hopelessness, pessimism, guilt,
worthlessness, helplessness, gloomy
Hard to be good enough, no one cares
Feeling empty in heart,
I've been hurt too many times
Unresolved life hurts and disappointments

Diabetes:
Judging self or others severely
Disappointed in life
Ongoing feelings of sorrow
Emotional shock
Joy of life is gone
Feeling "It should have been different"
Obsessed with wanting to control

Diarrhea:
Rejecting the visualization of something you don't want to accept
Wanting to be done with someone or something
Running away from a situation
Fear of something in the present
Obsessed with order

Dissociative Identity Disorder: (Multiple Personality)
Distrust, fear of getting hurt, no one is safe
Will not let my guard down
Life is frightening, unpredictable, unsafe
Don't let anyone too close, keep my distance
Unresolved past trauma

Dizziness:
Feeling overloaded
Feeling "I don't want to cope anymore"
Not wanting to accept things as they are
Unresolved anger, built up resentment
Carrying others burdens

Dry Eye:
Unable to express grief
Feelings turned off
Incorrect perceptions from early years;
keeping tears from flowing

Dysentery:
Fear of the present
Feelings of being unjustly dealt with

Dysmenorrhea:
Feelings of anger toward self
Inability to forgive self

Ears:
Hearing corresponds to the understanding
Hearing problems: Trying to force someone to hear things your way
What are the advantages of not hearing?

Earache:
Feelings of anger at what you are hearing
Don't want to hear what is going on
Children: Can't abide the turmoil in home

Eating Disorder:
Fear of being out of control
Don't feel good about myself
Must be perfect, I feel ugly
Past trauma unresolved
Unloved, not cared for
Not good enough for others
People too controlling

Eczema:
Over-sensitive
Feel you are being interfered with or prevented from doing something, thus feeling frustrated
Unresolved hurt feelings
Unresolved feelings of irritation

Edema:
Sympathy for self - keeping person from moving too fast
Body's way of putting on a cast
Feeling need to be immobilized in some area of body
Holding on to something that is not necessary

Elimination Problems:
Deep subconscious resentments
Holding on to past experiences
Not letting go, which creates blockages
Tension built up

Emotionless:
Afraid to express emotions
No one understands me
Not allowed to speak my mind
My feelings are not good enough
Past trauma unresolved

Emphysema:
Feeling unworthy to live
Fears taking in life to the fullest

Endometriosis:
Deep-seeded unresolved sadness going unanswered
Feelings of frustration
Feelings of insecurity
Lack of self-love
Wanting to blame problems on others

Epilepsy:
Overwhelmed with life
Need to persecute self
Wanting to reject life
Violence against self

Eyes:
Circles under:
Bitterness, remorse/regret
Self-condemnation, deep seeded grief
Feeling unfulfilled
Resentment/hurt

Watery:
Unable to express an inner grief
Not wanting to understand what you are seeing
Not seeing the truth
Fearing the future
Not wanting to see life as it is
Life is weak and out of focus
Not seeing eye to eye with another
Not forgiving
Inability to see one's own self-worth

Fainting:
Fear of the present
Feeling unable to cope
An excuse to blank out

Fallopian Tubes: (Blocked)
Nervous tension of long duration
High-strung temperament

Farsightedness:
Suppressed anger, focused outward in life

Fast Thinking: (Racing mind)
Mind will not stop thinking
My life has been taken from me
Feel dumb, stupid, less than others
Cannot fit into this world
Not feeling good about myself
Not allowed to think for myself
Must prove myself

Fatigue:
Resisting life, feeling bored

Not enjoying your place in life
Experiencing "burn out" in one's job or relationship

Fears-enclosed Places: (Claustrophobia)

Afraid to be out of control
Afraid bad things will happen
Cannot control situation
Emotion takes over
Unresolved past trauma

Fear of Relationship Commitment:

Fear of being emotionally hurt
Cannot get too close emotionally
Unresolved issues of rejection, abandonment,
relationship loss, separation, disappointment
In past- discouraged to love or be loved

Feet:

Fear of the future
Fear of stepping forward in life
Lack of understanding in many aspects of life

Female Problems:

Emotional block about sexuality
Feeling inadequate in sexual role
Feelings of fear or guilt about sex
Refusing to "let go" of the past
Feels to reject feminine nature

Fever:

Anger unable to be expressed
Feelings of resistance
Emotionally "burning up" about something
Being affected by lack of order
Holding on to the past

Fibroid Tumors and Cysts:

The ego has been injured
Unexpressed and unresolved hurts

Fibromyalgia:

Exhausted, working to be good enough
Need to be perfect, what would others think
Distrust of others, must be careful to do it right
Guilt, self denial, stuck in life, victim mentality
Must be careful with feelings, hold in everything
Unresolved past trauma

Fingers:
Fussing over details of life
Thumb: Affected by worry, depression, hate, anxiety, guilt and self-protection
Index: Affected by fear and resentment
Middle: Affected by anger, bitterness and sexuality
Ring: Affected by grief, inability to flow with life
Little: Affected by pretense, deceit and unforgiveness

Flu:
Fear, belief in mass negativity
Belief in the worst happening to you

Frigidity:
Unresolved fears, resentments or guilt having to do with sex and sexual relationships
Fixations, complexes or neurotic attachments affecting emotional nature

Fungus:
Inability to *let go* of the past
Allowing the past to rule the now

Gallbladder:
Resentment, galled, stubborn, repressed, hopelessness, incapable, depresssed
Feelings of bitterness and anger
Wanting to force things

Gallstones:
Feelings of bitterness and condemnation
Being unyielding, unforgiving, prideful
Withdrawn, depressed, grieving life

Gangrene:
Morbidity running wild
Unresolved poisonous feelings
Lack of self-love, insecurity

Gastritis:
Feelings of uncertainty and anxiety
Catastrophic thoughts and dread

Glandular Problems:
Long term inappropriate feelings
Unresolved feelings that have created gross imbalance

Glaucoma:
Hostility, unforgiveness,
Unresolved hurts, disappointments
Refusing to see what is ahead

Goiter:
Feeling unfulfilled and *being used*
Feel purposes have been thwarted

Gout:
Judging others harshly
Feelings of impatience
Feelings of anger held inside
Rejecting others or world around you
Wanting to dominate

Grave's Disease:
Driven to excel, perfectionism
Feeling undeserving of love
Anger from rejection, being unloved

Growths:
False sense of pride
Unresolved anger and resentments
Inability to accept Divine help
Spiritual understanding and values out of balance
Nursing buried hurts

Gum Problems:
No joy or fulfillment, afraid of failure
Unable to make decisions

Hands:
Has to do with the ability to grasp or let go of ideas
Left: Receiving or being passive
Right: Giving, reaching out or acting aggressively
Fearing new ideas and lack of opportunities
Hands have the ability to give or grab; explore or push away, hold on to let go; caress or punch

Hands – Arthritis:
Rigid, perfectionist or controlling personality
Severe self-criticism and criticism of others
Inflexible feelings repressed- mirrored in the hands

Hands – Cramps:
Conflict over ability and how to communicate it
Feels unable to communicate well verbally

Hands – Sweaty:
Fears making mistakes
Fears appearing incompetent or foolish

Hay Fever:
Unresolved feelings of rage or fear
Unresolved feelings of grief or sadness
Repressed tears held back
Repressed aggression
Wanting to *get even*
Feelings of guilt

Headaches:
Tension and stress
Inability to resolve emotional upsets
Hurt feelings going unexpressed
Feelings of inner pressure working on you
Feeling unable to control
Feelings of fear and anxiety getting the best of you
Unpleasant relationships
Inability to face an issue
Manifesting the need to laugh, sing, praise and express gratitude

Heart Problems:
Imbalanced joy, lack of emotion,
Violating the laws of love; knowingly or unknowingly
Feelings of compassion or rejection being blocked
Feelings of resentment and/or hurt
Not feeling approval from others
Upsetting family problems
Has a difficult time forgiving (including self)
Wanting to release from responsibility
In a relationship that hurts
Abnormal or inappropriate laughing, rapid mannerisms and speech, intolerance, arrogance

Hemorrhoids:
On-going feelings of being burdened
Feeling pressured or anxious
Feeling fear or tension
Inability to *let go*

Hepatitis:
Resistance to change, resentment
Feelings of anger, fear, hate

Hernia:
Feelings of anger, being burdened
Punishing self, emotionally unavailable
Unresolved hurt from past relationships

Herpes:
Feelings of guilt, shame, anxiety, anger

Herpes-Simplex:
Wanting to speak words of bitterness
Wanting to complain royally

Hips:
Fears making major decisions
Has nothing to look forward to
Lack of emotional and physical self-support

Hip-Joint:
Not wanting to accept present experiences
Non-acceptance of physical experiences

Hives:
Small hidden fears
Fears that are finally surfacing
Feeling mistreated
Inability to view things with the correct perspective
Anger – perceiving someone has inflexible behavior
Wanting to protest but unable to

Hodgkin's Disease:
Frantic need to feel accepted
Inability to accept self
Feels a continual need to prove self

Hoarding:
Abandonment issues
No one loves me
Feeling empty, sad, unfulfilled
Grieving, sad, strive to be happy
Afraid of losing everything
Search for identity, purpose, intimacy
Unresolved past hurt and loss

Huntington's Disease:
Resentment for inability to change others
Hopelessness, helplessness, deep sorrow

Hyperactivity:
Always wanting needs to be met but feels helpless to have it happen
Frustrated due to inability to feel peace

Hyperthyroidism:
Feelings of rage for being over looked

Hyperventilation:
Distrusting the flow of life
Feelings of resistance to life and it's uncertainties

Hypoglycemia:
Feelings of overwhelmed burdens
Feeling a lack of joy in life

Hypothalamus:
Feelings of: rage, insecurity, displeasure,
sadness, and anxiety

Immune System:
Giving up
Inability to care (feeling) for others
Feeling that "everything is out of my control"
Feeling "there's no use trying anymore"
Feeling of "I'm not enough"

Impotence:
Conflicting ideas about sex
Fear, resentments or guilt having to do with sex and sexual relationships
Unresolved fears towards mother
Psychic obsessions or sexual frustration
Emotional nature affected by complexes, fixations or neurotic attachments

Incontinence:
Weary of controlling the emotions
Overflowing emotions

Indigestion:
Feeling everyone is against you
Feel you need to fight your way through life
Feelings of anxiety
Fear of losing job; losing security

Infection:
Feelings of hostility, anger being manifested,
suspicion or annoyance

Inflammation:
Feelings of rage, anger, anxiety about life

Influenza:
Believing the worst will happen to you
Fearing the worst

Insomnia:
Tensions in life, deep seeded guilt
Feelings of fear and anxiety
Reaction to potential threatening situations

Intestinal Diseases:
Inability to assimilate and absorb the new in life
Wanting to live in the past
Desire to stay in *comfort zone*
Constipation, bloating, hernia, thoraco-lumbar pain, abdominal pain, hemor-
rhoids, flatulence
Dogmatic, crying, compelled to neatness, fear of rejection, financial worries,
defensive

Itching:
Desires gone unfulfilled
Difficulty accepting where you are in life
Wanting more out of life

Jaw Problems: (TMJ Syndrome)
Feelings of rage
Subconsciously wanting revenge
Inability to express how one feels

Joints:
Feelings of resentment
Suppressing hurt feelings

Kidney Problems:
Unresolved fear, dread,
Extension of bladder but more severe
Insensitive to situations where caring and concerning should be exhibited
Trying to control life
Being over-judgmental
Feeling emotional confusion

Deep subconscious resentments toward people and experiences of the past
Unfounded criticism of others
Paralyzed will, hostility, obsessive, feeling of shame, contemplation

Kidney Stones:
Hardened anger, negative thinking
Suppressed emotions
Unable to get close emotionally

Knee Problems:
Unable to be flexible
Not wanting to bend, usually to authority
Ego and/or pride gets in the way
Stubborn: wanting own way

Knee – Left:
Need to be more receptive to events
Feelings of insecurity
Experiencing unresolved stress

Knee – Right:
Need to be more assertive
Not wanting to *give in* to authority

Large Intestine:
Dogmatic, crying, compelled to neatness,
Fear of rejection, financial worries, defensive

Laryngitis:
Fears voicing opinions
Resentment toward authority
Repressed emotions and fears
Gripped anger
Irritation at someone or a situation

Left Side of Body:
Feminine side/Represents receiving
Leg Problems:
Fear of moving ahead with life
Fear of change
Has difficulty in being resolute about issues
Inability to understand

Leg Paralysis:
Avoiding situation you don't life
Avoiding something you are afraid of

Leukemia:
Feelings of deep depression
Feelings of anger or ill will
Loss of a parent or a career position
Feelings of total helplessness
Giving up or quitting
Unable to express emotions
Present/future conditions are intolerable
Feelings of despair

Leukorrhea:
Sexual guilt
Feeling powerless
Feeling anger toward mate

Lou Gehrig 's Disease: (ALS)
Unwillingness to accept self-worth
Denial of success

Liver: (Anger Center)
Unresolved anger
Irrational, frustration, unforgiveness,
Resentment and pettiness
Being judgmental
Critical thoughts
Not forgiving self and others
Feelings of injustice and revenge
Self-condemnation, possessive
Regret over the past/sadness

Lock Jaw:
Feelings of rage
Wanting to control
Inability to express feelings

Lungs:
Unresolved feelings of grief, sadness
Not feeling approval, unappreciated
Hurts where love is concerned
Feels life is monotonous
Cloudy thinking, anguish,
resistance to accepting love

Lupus:
Deep-seeded grief
Feels like "giving up"
Laughing on outside, crying on inside

Lymphatic Vessels:
Breaking the laws of love
Breaking the laws of peace and joy
Resentment, hatred or anger

Lymph System:
Lack of enthusiasm
Unable to feel acceptance

Mastoiditis: (Most often in children)
Not wanting to hear what is happening
Fears that affect understanding
Feeling left out

Menopause:
Fears this time of life and getting older
Fears being rejected
Feeling useless

Menstrual Problems:
Unresolved feelings of guilt
Fears role as a woman
Feels no joy in being a woman

Migraine Headaches:
Unable to flow easily with life
Want to take things at own pace
Dislikes being pushed
Inability to handle pressure or stress
Pushing to control; wants to control

Miscarriage:
Fears timing is "wrong"
Fears what the future will bring
Fears the responsibility of baby

Mononucleosis:
Feeling unloved and unworthy
Anger from not being appreciated

Motion Sickness:
Fears not having control

Mouth problems:
Resistant to change
Fears moving out of *comfort zone*
Opinionated

Multiple Sclerosis:
Unwilling to be flexible
Unreceptive to new ideas
Hard on self: blames self
Incorrect use of will
Unforgiving of self or others

Muscle Cramps:
Stubborn nature, a willful attitude
Resists moving forward in life

Muscular-Skeletal Diseases: (Muscular Dystrophy)
A form of self-created paralysis to keep from hitting someone or moving forward
Deep-seeded anger that has not been resolved
Feels "I must experience pain"

Myasthenia Gravis:
Laughing on outside, but crying on inside
Helplessness to change conditions
Deep-seeded grief
Feels like giving up
Fears a change in life

Nail-biting:
Unfulfilled desires
Feeling spiteful towards parents
Feelings of frustration

Narcolepsy:
Wishing you were somewhere else
Don't want to cope anymore
Weary of responsibilities
Wishing responsibilities would go away

Nausea:
Rejecting what you don't want to see
Wishing an undesirable situation never happened
Fear of something about to happen

Nearsightedness:
Childhood fear, difficult looking at immediate issues

Neck Problems:
Moving under pressure
Want to let feelings out but don't dare
Inflexible state of mind
Not wanting to yield to opinions you think are wrong
Non-acceptance and rejection of others

Nephritis:
Feelings of disappointment
Feelings of failure, life is unfair

Nerves:
Influenced by thoughts and feelings
How the body communicates within
Parasympathetic: Holding on to things or people of the past that need releasing

Nervous Breakdown:
Inability to communicate true feelings
Fear of the future

Nervousness:
Inability to communicate feelings adequately
Fear of the future, feelings of anxiety
Confused thinking

Neuritis:
Feeling of being irritated without your consent
Your power is negated because of being irritated

Neuropathy:
Feelings are unacceptable and repressed
Retreating from life, distrust emotions

Neurosis:
Overload; pressures too hard to bear
No letting up; "can't quit"

Nodules:
Feelings of frustration and resentment
Feel you always have to prove yourself
Ego feels in jeopardy

Nose:
Bleeds: Feeling overlooked
Runny: Crying on the inside; wanting help
Running away from unwanted responsibility

Stuffy: Not accepting your worth
Desire for love

Numbness:
Not expressing love or consideration

Obesity:
Using food as a substitute for affection
Inability to admit what you really want
Inability to express true feelings
Seeking love, protecting the body
Trying to fulfill the self
Stuffed feelings

Obsessive-Compulsive: (Acts-Thoughts)
Afraid something bad will happen
Fear of being sick or contaminated
Fear of causing harm to self or others
Must be perfect, not good enough
Unloved, no one cares
Deep hurt of abandonment
Unresolved past hurt from others

Osteomyelitis:
Feeling a lack of support
Feeling frustrated and angry with life

Ovaries:
Feelings of loneliness
Desire to feel love and respect
Feeling inadequate in sexual role

Overweight:
Feelings of insecurity
Feelings of self-rejection
Wanting to protect the body
Seeking love and fulfillment
Attempting to fulfill the self
Feelings are being stuffed inside
Unexpressed, mis-perceived and inappropriate feelings

Palsy:
Feeling stagnant in life
Feel you can't move forward in life

Pancreas:
Feelings of judgment, guilt, low self-esteem
Suppressing laughter
Incorrect use of ego
Feels the joy of living is gone/not allowing joy

Panic Attacks:
Overwhelming fear
Neglect, abandonment, fear
Feeling of no control, must make it right
Afraid something bad will happen
Afraid of dying, lack of trust
Unresolved past trauma

Paralysis:
Feeling overwhelmed by responsibilities
Sub-consciously wanting to escape
Resisting life and fear of the future

Paralyzed Arms:
Left arm: Difficulty in receiving from others
Right arm: Difficulty in giving to others
Resistance to an unexplained hardness of will
Tension of the mind

Paranoia:
Afraid to trust others
Fear of being hurt
Cannot forgive
Anyone can hurt you
Afraid to get close
Hurt by important people
Unresolved past trauma

Parasites:
Feelings rule you rather than ruling feelings

Parathyroid:
Unresolved anger

Parkinson's Disease:
Wanting full control
Fears not being able to control
Feeling unsafe and uncared for

Pelvis:
Unable to remain grounded or focused in emotional activity
Relates to holding on to sexual feelings

Peptic Ulcer:
Feels a lack of self-worth
Responsible for pleasing everyone

Phlebitis:
Feeling trapped, *no way out*
Life's problems can't be solved

Phobias:
Fear, dread something bad will happen
Not feeling safe, cannot trust
Not protected, not loved
Important people not there for me
Afraid of losing control
Unresolved past trauma

Pineal Gland:
Corresponds with inner seeing and hearing
Refusing to receive understanding and enlightenment, misusing faith
Discouragement, lost direction, intuition, motivation, imagination, enlightenment, energy, out of balance

Pink-Eye:
Feelings of frustration
Feelings of anger at present situation
Wanting to obscure what is going on around you

Pituitary Gland:
Always picturing ill health or sickness
Constant recipient of bad luck/misfortune
Not able to see good in things

Plantar Wart:
Frustrated about life and the future
Deep seeded anger

Pneumonia:
Weary of life
Unresolved emotional hurts
Feelings of desperation

Pleurisy:
Feeling antagonism and hostility

Post-Nasal Drip:
Crying on inside, inner grief
Feeling as a *victim*

Premenstrual Syndrome: (PMS)
Relinquishing power to others
Rejecting the feminine aspect of self
Anger and despair

Prostate Problems:
Ideas are in conflict about sex
Refusing to *let go* of the past
Fear of aging
Feels like *throwing in the towel*
Suppressed emotions, non-thinking, non-emotive, depleted, vivid dreaming, sexually focused, sluggish memory, selfishness, greed – at the expense of others

Prostate Cancer:
Repressed anger at being restricted

Psoriasis:
Emotional insecurity
Unwilling to be accountable for own feelings
Unresolved, deep-seeded hurt feelings surfacing

Pyorrhea:
Angry at self for not making decisions

Rage – Explosive Fits:
Angry at world, must prove self
People not emotionally there
Afraid to show true feelings
Unloved, abuse, and strict up bring
Not good enough
Cannot trust or get close
Hurt others before getting hurt
Unresolved past trauma

Rash:
Being irritated by something or someone
Unable to flow with life

Respiratory Problems:
Not feeling approval, lack of love
Fears living life to the fullest

Restless Leg Syndrome:
Must have complete control
Anger, hurt when has no control

Rheumatism:
Resentment and wanting revenge
"I am a victim" syndrome
Long-standing bitterness
Has a problem loving self and others

Right-Left Split:
Right: Masculine side/Fighting/Giving/Releasing side
Left: Feminine side/Protecting/Receiving/Taking side

Sacroiliac Problems:
Feel you're in the *wrong* place (job, city, relationship, etc.)

Sciatica:
Mental anxieties regarding creative abilities
Sexual abnormality or frustration
Over-concerned with money issues
Being double-minded

Seizures:
Feel pressure, overwhelmed
Fear, despair, angry re: situation
Running away from self and life

Separation Anxiety:
Afraid of abandonment
Afraid to be alone
No one cares about me
Deep hurt from past trauma
Unresolved past emotion

Sex Organs:
Feelings of apathy, separated

Shins:
Not being true to ideals and values

Shingles:
Fear things won't work out the way we want
Over-sensitive
On-going tension concerning a situation
Hostile energy being manifest

Shoulders: (Our expressive part)
Bearing burdens of others
Life is too great burden to bear
Carrying stressful responsibilities
Lacking in courage
Hunched and sloped: Feels life is a tough struggle
Round: Feelings of hopeless/helpless
Scoliosis: Inability to trust life

Sickle Cell Anemia:
Feeling inferiority, unloved, past hurts

Sinus Trouble:
Trying to *call the shots* in someone else's life
Dominating possessive
Irritated by people close to you

Skin Disease:
Unresolved feelings of irritation
Unresolved feelings of criticism
Disturbed over trivial things
Lack of security
Feeling impatience, bored, unsettled

Skin Rashes:
Inner conflicts surfacing
Someone or something is irritating you
Frustrated not able to accomplish things

Sleep Apnea:
Disappointment, unforgiveness, bitter
Fear of rejection, unloved as child

Small Intestine:
Lost, vulnerable, abandoned, deserted, absent-mindedness, insecurity, attachment profoundly deep unrequited love

Snoring:
Refusal to eliminate old patterns
Unresolved past hurts, blamed

Sore-Throat:
Feelings of anger going unexpressed
Other negative feelings going unexpressed

Spasms: Thoughts, feelings of fear

Spastic Colon: (Irritable Bowel Syndrome)
Insecurity, poor support now or past
Unable to *let go* and flow with life

Spine: (Has to do with the ego)
Ego getting carried away in pride
Feelings of shyness and inferiority

Spinal Meningitis:
Unresolved feelings of rage
Inflammatory thoughts

Spleen:
Lack of self-love
Unable to feel love, rejected
Emotional conflicts
Feeling intense anger/antagonism
Worry, low self-esteem, lack of control, overly sympathetic, uncertainty, deprived of the sweet things in life, brooding

Sprains:
Feelings of resistance
Inability to change directions in life

Sterility:
Extreme nervous tension
Hard and cold in attitudes

Stiffness:
Inability to give
Inflexible in opinions and attitudes

Stomach Cancer:
Wanting to get even, spite
Wanting revenge

Stomach Problems:
Our security feels threatened
Fears new ideas
Lack of affection, unhappy

Condemning success of others
Nervous, disgust, impatience
Obsession with things

Stuttering:
Dares not protest feelings
Unable to express self
Emotionally insecure
Needing to please

Stroke:
Rejecting life at a deep level
Extreme resistance, self-violence
Overloaded with pressures of life
Feel like *giving up*

Sty:
Not seeing the best in another person
Unresolved feelings of anger toward someone

Suicidal:
Feeling totally unable to resolve life's problems
Feeling there is no hope for tomorrow
Feeling "What's the use"
Feels "Everyone would be better off without me"

Swelling:
Holding on to negative feelings

Tailbone:
Unduly concerned with material needs and survival needs

Teeth: (Painful)
Inability to be decisive

Tendons: (Knots In)
Mental poisons
Unwilling to accept full stature
Need to forgive self

Throat:
Restrained anger and feelings
Critical words spoken
Holding in emotional hurts
Not having own way
Feeling of confusion

Lack of discernment
Knowledge used unwisely

Thrush:
Anger from incorrect choices

Thymus:
Persecuted, picked on,
Life is unfair, unprotected

Thyroid:
Fears self-expression
Frustration/anxiety
Lack of discernment
Paranoia, muddled thinking,
Instability, "can't figure it out"

Tinnitus:
Refusing to hear ones *inner voice*
Not wanting to listen to high laws

TMJ:
Repressed anger, distrust, anxiety
Frustrated with life, high expectations

Toes:
Worrying about minor details

Tongue:
Not speaking truth
Inability to taste beauty, joy of life

Tonsils:
Tense will
Repressed fear or anger
Irritation at someone or something
Not getting own way

Tuberculosis:
Continual selfishness
Feeling possessive
Being cruel to others

Tumors: (False Growth)
Suppressed hurts, remorse
Unresolved hate and anger

False values and pride
Unforgiveness and resentment
Doesn't feel close to parents
Forgiveness and love are healing

Ulcers:
Worrying over details
Things not going your way
Pressures too much to bear
Anxiety, fear or tension
Seeking revenge
Helplessness, powerlessness

Underweight:
Worries, fears, distrusting life
Feeling extreme tension

Urinary Infections:
Putting blame on others for your problems
Allowing another to irritate you

Uterine Cancer:
Being ticked off at the male gender
Repressed anger, feeling like a martyr

Uterus:
Has to do with unresolved feelings towards mother
Negative feelings toward creative aspect of life

Vaginitis:
Sexual guilt, need to punish self
Loss of loved one or something

Varicose Veins:
Pronounced tension
Wanting to *run away*
Discouragement, overburdened
Negativity and resistance

Venereal Disease:
Feels a need to be punished
Guilty about sexual activities

Viral Infections:
Bitterness and ugliness overshadowing the beautiful and good in life
Belief, "I get everything that comes along"

Vomiting:
Rejecting things you don't want to accept
Feelings of disgust

Warts:
Refusing to see the beauty in life
Feelings of hate taking form

Yeast Infections:
Unresolved hurts, resentments
Lack of self-love
Inability to claim your power
Unable to love and support self
Unable to accept self
Not recognizing own needs

REFERENCES

References are taken from Craig's years of clinical observation and with grateful appreciation, taken from the following copyrighted material:

1. Karol Truman, *Feelings Buried Alive Never Die* . . . (St. George, UT: Olympus Publishers, 1991), 220-64.

2. *Reflex Emotional Therapies,* (Portland, OR, Professional Complementary Health Formulas, 2001).

3. *Diagnostic Statistical Manual of Mental Disorders IV,* (Washington, DC: American Psychiatric Association, 1994).

4. Michael J. Lincoln, *Messages from the Body: Their Psychological Meaning* (Cool, CA: Talking Hearts, 2006).

Appendix I

FIVE-STEP PRAYER MODEL

This Global Awakening Five-Step Prayer Model is a way to pray for healing and has been taught and used by ministry teams at Global Awakening conference, crusades, and international trips bearing powerful fruit in people's lives. It is quiet, loving, and effective. It can be used by anyone and anywhere-in the home; in the gathering of believers; and for reaching out in the streets, marketplace, and workplace!

1. Interview – After you notice a condition

What is your name?

How long have you had this condition? Do you know the cause?

Determine the root cause of the infirmity or sickness.

Possible roots: Afflicting spirit; often emotionally rooted or natural causes (i.e., injury, or disease)

Ask probing questions:

Do you have a doctor's diagnosis?

Did someone cause this condition? Have you forgiven him/her?

Did any significant event happen to you within a year before this condition started? (Before praying- the person may need help with unforgiveness or emotional wounds, i.e., fear, shame, or rejection.)

Depend on Holy Spirit – ask H/S about the condition or its cause. Listen to Him!

2. Prayer Selection

USING PETITION (when progress has stopped) – "Father, in Jesus' name I ask You to heal the inflammation in Joe's knee and take out the swelling and pain."

TYPICALLY USE COMMAND – "In the name of Jesus I command the inflammation in Joe's knee to be healed and all swelling and pain to leave."

Use this to break a curse or vow or to cast out an afflicting spirit or other spirit

A word of knowledge indicates that God wants to heal the person immediately.

3. Prayer Ministry

Audibly ask Holy Spirit to be present with His guidance and His healing power.

Ask the person not to pray but instead, to close his eyes and focus on his body.

Ask person to tell you if they feel something: heat/electricity/trembling, etc.

Keep your eyes open, to see God's touch

Use short, specific prayers following any leading of Holy Spirit

Try different kinds of prayer as you are loving! Always pray in the name of Jesus

Don't preach or give advice

If a specific prayer brings improvement, keep using it immediately - Be persistent!

Pray for symptom and cause, if cause is known. Periodically ask, "What's going on?"

Remember: trust Holy Spirit, not the method

Thank God for whatever He does (you cannot thank God too much!)

4. Stop and Re-interview after prayer—Ask, "What is going on?"

If their condition feels better, ask, "What percentage of better to you feel, 10 percent, 20 percent, etc.

If pain moves around or increases during prayer or if a condition has existed a long time, consider casting out an afflicting spirit.

If you are not making progress, consider interviewing the person further:

Would you try again to remember any significant event?

Have any other members of your family ever had this condition?

Do you have a strong fear of anything?

Has anyone ever pronounced a curse over you or your family?

Do you know of anyone who is very angry at you?

Have you ever participated in any kind of satanic or other occult activity?

Has anyone in your family been a member of the freemasons?

Have you had other accidents? (He or she may be accident-prone.)

Review hindrances to healing

Stop praying when:

The person: a) is healed; or b) wants you to stop; or c) Holy Spirit tells you to stop; or d) you are gaining no ground and receive no other way to pray.

5. Post-prayer Suggestions:

After praying, it is beneficial to give helpful follow-up instructions or exhortations:

Encourage the person with Scripture

If someone is not healed or is only partially healed, do NOT accuse the person of a lack of faith or of sin in his or her life as the cause

Give information about how to keep their healing

© *Adapted from 2010 Global Awakening*

Appendix II

PRAYER FOR DELIVERANCE

The objective is to expel any demons, close their avenues of access to the victim, and enable him to keep those avenues closed in the future. It is most effective to work as a team. One person is in charge, he or she does all the talking and, in steps 2, 6, 7 and 8, all the touching. Others pray silently and talk with the leader quietly. Leadership can rotate during ministry. Steps 6 and 7 can be extremely painful. Don't hesitate to stop, provide comfort, and pray for healing. If the person can't remember important details or identify the cause of feelings, you can interrupt the ministry time and have him go home and ask the Holy Spirit.

1. Give the individual priority. Maintain a loving attitude. Be encouraging. Move to a quiet place if possible. Invite the Holy Spirit to be present.

2. If a spirit manifests, make it be quiet. Repeat "Submit in the name of Jesus!" Be persistent, this may take time. Only the leader touches the person.

3. Establish and maintain communication with the person. You must have his cooperation. "Joe, can you hear me? Look at me!"

4. Ask the person what he or she wants freedom from. Make sure he or she really wants freedom from the bondage(s).

5. Make sure the person has accepted Jesus as Lord and Savior. If not, lead him in prayer for salvation. If you can't, bless him but don't try deliverance.

6. Interview the person to discover the event(s) or relationship(s) that have led to the bondage(s). Expose where forgiveness is required, and where healing, repentance and breaking of bondages are needed. Find all open doors. If there is no obvious place to start, begin with his or her parental relationships, then move to other areas. Be thorough, don't rush. Do not stir up demons, keep them quiet. List the spirits encountered and areas requiring forgiveness of others or repentance. Consider a curse if the person has persistent difficulty in an area of life. Fear is an entry point for different spirits and a problem in many illnesses.

7. Lead the person in closing the door(s) through which the spirit(s) entered (If there is no one to forgive, go to Steps B through D.)

He or she should:

A. "Forgive whoever caused the hurt or led him or her into wrong conduct. Be specific, item-by-item. The seeker should release the offender to God, and commit to take his or her hands off—to not try to change the offender, and ask God to bless him or her in every way. If the seeker is unable to forgive, explain the scripture to him or her. You can quietly bind any spirit of unforgiveness. if he or she is still unable to forgive, pray for healing and blessing but not deliverance.

B. Repent of his or her specific sins in the situation(s). "Father, forgive me for _____ (hate, bitterness, sharing my body with _____, reading horoscopes, etc.")

C. Renounce audibly and firmly all spirits involved, in the name of Jesus. In the case of sex outside marriage, the person should renounce spirits taken in from every partner he or she can recall, individually by first names. Pacts with satan and inner vows must be renounced and curses broken. "In the name of Jesus I renounce the spirits of _____ and _____." "In the name of Jesus, I renounce the vow I made never/always to _____."

D. Break the bondage(s) caused by the sin, attitude, conduct, vow, spirit, curse, etc. In the name of Jesus. This closes the door. (You or the seeker can do this.) "In the name of Jesus I break the power of the spirit(s) of _____ over ((Tom) so that when they are cast out, they will not come back." "In the name of Jesus I break the power of every curse over (Tom) from _____ (Father's careless critical words, father's freemasonry, etc.)"

8. Cast out the unclean spirit(s) in the name of Jesus. Some people cast spirits out one-by-one, some cast them out by groups. Do what works for you. With all doors closed, the spirits will leave quickly and quietly. If they don't leave promptly, go back to Step 6. Tell the person there may be other spirits to deal with. Re-interview. Ask the Holy Spirit to show you or the seeker or a team member what He wants to do next. He is very willing to help you!

9. Have the person thank Jesus for his or her deliverance. If he or she cannot, or if spirits manifest, more doors need to be closed.

10. Have the person ask the Holy Spirit to fill him or her and all the places formerly occupied by the evil spirits.

© 2010 Global Awakening

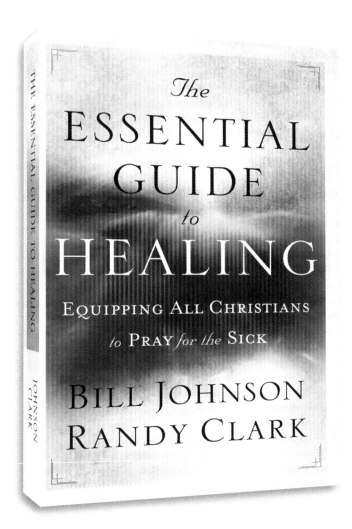

YOU CAN HEAL THE SICK TOO!

For the first time, premier renewal leaders Bill Johnson and Dr. Randy Clark team up to equip Christians to minister healing. Grounded from start to finish in Scripture, Johnson and Clark lay out the rich theological and historical foundation for healing in the church today. Full of inspiring stories, this book offers practical, proven, step-by-step guidance to ministering healing. The ministry of healing is not reserved for a select few. God's miraculous healing is part of the Good News--and every believer can become a conduit for his healing power.

FOR THIS AND OTHER BOOKS GO TO: GLOBALAWAKENINGSTORE.COM

THE CORE MESSAGE SERIES

FROM RANDY CLARK

Awed By His Grace / Out of the Bunkhouse

Baptism in the Holy Spirit

Biblical Basis for Healing

Christ in You the Hope of Glory / Healing and the Glory

Evangelism Unleashed

Healing is in the Atonement / Power of the Lord's Supper

Healing Out of Intimacy / Acts of Obedience

Learning to Minister Under the Anointing /
Healing Ministry in Your Church

Open Heaven / Are You Thirsty

Pressing In / Spend and Be Spent

Thrill of Victory / Agony of Defeat

Words of Knowledge

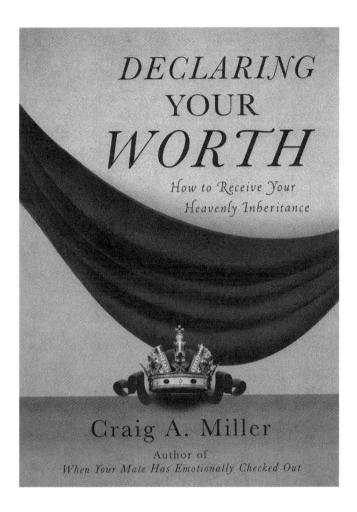

DECLARING YOUR WORTH
Book & Audio CD

If you like to read about miracles and become encouraged about your authority and power from God, this devotional is for you! Each short chapter has an inspiring miracle story, practical instructions about healing, and powerful declarations over yourself based on scriptures to declare that you are: worthy, lovable, significant, blameless, accepted, forgiven, set free, victorious, purposeful, confident, attractive, hopeful, blessed, and much more. Tate Publishing, paperback, 90 pages

Available through:

www.feelingsbook.com (available in paperback, audio CD)
www.amazon.com (available in kindle, paperback, audio CD)

OTHER RESOURCES

FROM CRAIG MILLER

WHEN YOUR MATE HAS EMOTIONALLY CHECKED OUT

(TATE PUBLISHING)

WHEN FEELINGS DON'T COME EASY

(AMERICA STAR BOOKS)

BETTER LIFE SPOTLIGHT

(DVD BY WLMB TV-40, TOLEDO, OH)

• •

For more details about the counseling ministry, Masterpeace Center for Counseling and Development, in Tecumseh, Michigan, go to, www.mpccd.com and for information about speaking engagements and resources, go to, www.feelingsbook.com